This journal belongs to

_____

"EACH TIME OF LIFE HAS ITS OWN KIND OF LOVE," wrote Tolstoy, and each time of life has its own kind of happiness. In the rush of everyday existence, however, it's easy for the small, sweet moments to be forgotten. I think, "I'll never forget that funny thing my daughter said," but I will, I will.

To help me remember these days, I decided to keep a one-sentence journal. I knew I'd never be able to write several daily pages in a proper journal, but I could write one sentence each night. And, I've found, one sentence is enough to hold on to the memories of the past. A one-sentence journal is satisfying because it's manageable; it gives a feeling of accomplishment; and it helps me reflect on and recall the experiences of parenthood.

With children, so much happens in just five years! It's extraordinary. A one-sentence journal is a simple way to preserve memories of this fleeting, precious time of life.

—*Gretchen Rubin, author of*
The Happiness Project *and* ***Happier at Home***

POTTER STYLE

Cover and interior design by Danielle Deschenes
Illustrations by Jacqueline Schmidt

www.clarksonpotter.com

ISBN 978-0-385-34865-2

Printed in China

JANUARY 1

"To be happy at home is the ultimate result of all ambition,
the end to which every enterprise and labour tends."

—*Samuel Johnson*

20 ___ * _____

_____

_____

20 ___ * _____

_____

_____

20 ___ * _____

_____

_____

20 ___ * _____

_____

_____

20 ___ * _____

_____

_____

2

JANUARY

To be happy, you need to think about
feeling good, feeling bad, and feeling right,
in an atmosphere of growth.

20 ⬤ * _____

_____

_____

20 ⬤ * _____

_____

_____

20 ⬤ * _____

_____

_____

20 ⬤ * _____

_____

_____

20 ⬤ * _____

_____

_____

JANUARY

How can you get more *feeling good*? More fun, more love, more energy. To be happy, it's not enough to eliminate the negative; you must also have sources of positive emotions.

20 ___ * _____

_____

_____

_____

20 ___ * _____

_____

_____

_____

20 ___ * _____

_____

_____

_____

20 ___ * _____

_____

_____

_____

20 ___ * _____

_____

_____

_____

4 JANUARY

What sources of *feeling bad* can you eliminate?
You can use negative feelings and painful pricks of
conscience to spotlight areas ripe for change.

20 ___ * _____
_____
_____

20 ___ * _____
_____
_____

20 ___ * _____
_____
_____

20 ___ * _____
_____
_____

20 ___ * _____
_____
_____

JANUARY

"The disturbers of happiness are our desires,
our griefs, and our fears."

—*Samuel Johnson*

20 ⬭⬭ * _____

_____

_____

_____

20 ⬭⬭ * _____

_____

_____

_____

20 ⬭⬭ * _____

_____

_____

_____

20 ⬭⬭ * _____

_____

_____

_____

20 ⬭⬭ * _____

_____

_____

_____

6 JANUARY

We want to *feel right* about our lives. Feeling right is a matter of virtue (doing your duty, living up to your own standards) and also about living the life that's right for you. To feel right, look for ways to make your home more closely reflect your values. Your ordinary routine should reflect the things most important to you.

20 ⬤ * _____

_____

_____

_____

20 ⬤ * _____

_____

_____

_____

20 ⬤ * _____

_____

_____

_____

20 ⬤ * _____

_____

_____

_____

20 ⬤ * _____

_____

_____

_____

JANUARY

"A man is not only happy but wise also, if he is trying, during his lifetime, to be the sort of man he wants to be found at his death."

— *Thomas à Kempis*

20 __ * _____

20 __ * _____

20 __ * _____

20 __ * _____

20 __ * _____

JANUARY

The process of striving after goals—that is, *growth*—brings happiness. If you want an atmosphere of growth to pervade your home, consider how you can make your surroundings more beautiful and functional.

20 ⬭ * _____

_____

_____

_____

20 ⬭ * _____

_____

_____

_____

20 ⬭ * _____

_____

_____

_____

20 ⬭ * _____

_____

_____

_____

20 ⬭ * _____

_____

_____

_____

JANUARY

"Happiness is neither virtue nor pleasure
nor this thing nor that, but simply growth.
We are happy when we are growing."

—William Butler Yeats

20 ___ * _____

_____

_____

_____

20 ___ * _____

_____

_____

_____

20 ___ * _____

_____

_____

_____

20 ___ * _____

_____

_____

_____

20 ___ * _____

_____

_____

_____

10 JANUARY

It takes work to be happier, but it's
gratifying work; the real challenge is to decide
purposely what to do—and then to *do* it.

20 ___ * _____

_____

_____

_____

20 ___ * _____

_____

_____

_____

20 ___ * _____

_____

_____

_____

20 ___ * _____

_____

_____

_____

20 ___ * _____

_____

_____

_____

JANUARY

Try choosing a single word or phrase as an overarching
theme for your entire year. When I decided to do this,
I knew exactly which word to choose as my theme: *Bigger*.
It would challenge me to think big, to tolerate
complications and failure, to expect more from myself.

20 ___ * _____

_____

_____

_____

20 ___ * _____

_____

_____

_____

20 ___ * _____

_____

_____

_____

20 ___ * _____

_____

_____

_____

20 ___ * _____

_____

_____

_____

12 JANUARY

In January, I wanted to cultivate an atmosphere of unhurriedness at home. I wanted plenty of time to get where I needed to go, to do the things that I wanted to do, with little time wasted on unsatisfying activities.

20 ___ * _____

_____

_____

_____

20 ___ * _____

_____

_____

_____

20 ___ * _____

_____

_____

_____

20 ___ * _____

_____

_____

_____

20 ___ * _____

_____

_____

_____

JANUARY 13

Home should calm you and energize you. It should
be a comforting, quiet refuge and a place of excitement
and possibility. By making you feel safe, it should
embolden you to take risks. Your home can be both
wading pool and diving board.

20 ___ * _____
_____
_____
_____

20 ___ * _____
_____
_____
_____

20 ___ * _____
_____
_____
_____

20 ___ * _____
_____
_____
_____

20 ___ * _____
_____
_____
_____

14 JANUARY

I sometimes wish I could forget about my resolutions.
I want to work, not visit the museum with my daughter.
I don't want to take the time to hold open the door
for the slow-walking woman or even to say a polite
"Hello" to the other parents at morning drop-off.

20 ___ * _____

_____

_____

20 ___ * _____

_____

_____

20 ___ * _____

_____

_____

20 ___ * _____

_____

_____

20 ___ * _____

_____

_____

JANUARY 15

"My mom says some days are like that. Even in Australia."

—*Judith Viorst*, **Alexander and the Terrible, Horrible, No Good, Very Bad Day**

20 * _____

_____

_____

_____

20 * _____

_____

_____

_____

20 * _____

_____

_____

_____

20 * _____

_____

_____

_____

20 * _____

_____

_____

_____

16 JANUARY

One of the best ways to make *yourself* happy is to
make *other people* happy; One of the best ways to make
other people happy is to be happy *yourself*.

20 ___ * _____

_____

_____

_____

20 ___ * _____

_____

_____

_____

20 ___ * _____

_____

_____

_____

20 ___ * _____

_____

_____

_____

20 ___ * _____

_____

_____

_____

JANUARY 17

While I might enjoy giving everyone assignments to make my family (and also myself) happier, in the end, I can change no one but myself. My desire for more affectionate gestures shouldn't become a focus of nagging, and my clutter-clearing zeal shouldn't justify a sneak purge of my daughter's dusty stuffed animals.

20 ____ * _____

_____

_____

_____

20 ____ * _____

_____

_____

_____

20 ____ * _____

_____

_____

_____

20 ____ * _____

_____

_____

_____

20 ____ * _____

_____

_____

_____

18 JANUARY

As Robert Frost wrote, home is "Something you somehow haven't to deserve." At home, I feel a greater sense of safety and acceptance, and also of responsibility and obligation. With friends, my hospitality is voluntary, but my family never needs an invitation.

20 ___ * _____

_____

_____

_____

20 ___ * _____

_____

_____

_____

20 ___ * _____

_____

_____

_____

20 ___ * _____

_____

_____

_____

20 ___ * _____

_____

_____

_____

JANUARY 19

Many things that most boosted my happiness also added complexity to my life. Having children. Learning to post videos to my website. Going to an out-of-town wedding. Applied too broadly, my impulse to "Keep it simple" would impoverish me.

20 ⬭ * _____

_____

_____

_____

20 ⬭ * _____

_____

_____

_____

20 ⬭ * _____

_____

_____

_____

20 ⬭ * _____

_____

_____

_____

20 ⬭ * _____

_____

_____

_____

20 JANUARY

While the term "happiness" might suggest a final, magical destination, the aim of a happiness project is not to achieve perfect "happiness," but rather to become *happier*. Next week, next year, what can you do to be happier?

20 ⬤ * _____

_____

_____

_____

20 ⬤ * _____

_____

_____

_____

20 ⬤ * _____

_____

_____

_____

20 ⬤ * _____

_____

_____

_____

20 ⬤ * _____

_____

_____

_____

JANUARY 21

At certain points in our lives, it's not possible to be happy, but it's possible to try to be *happier*, as happy as we can be, under the circumstances, and by doing so, fortify ourselves against adversity.

20 __ *

20 __ *

20 __ *

20 __ *

20 __ *

22 JANUARY

Because I know I'll be happier if I make time to tackle the chores I dread, I've resolved to "Suffer for fifteen minutes" each day on a long-postponed task; this is an unenjoyable resolution, but after all, happiness doesn't always make me *feel* happy.

20 ___ * _____

_____

_____

_____

20 ___ * _____

_____

_____

_____

20 ___ * _____

_____

_____

_____

20 ___ * _____

_____

_____

_____

20 ___ * _____

_____

_____

_____

JANUARY 23

Working at a task for just fifteen minutes a day showed me how much I could accomplish when I did a manageable amount of work, on a regular basis. As Anthony Trollope, observed, "A small daily task, if it be really daily, will beat the labors of a spasmodic Hercules."

20 ___ * _____

_____

_____

_____

20 ___ * _____

_____

_____

_____

20 ___ * _____

_____

_____

_____

20 ___ * _____

_____

_____

_____

20 ___ * _____

_____

_____

_____

24 JANUARY

Home is a state of mind,
but it's also a physical experience.

20 ___ * _____
_____
_____
_____

20 ___ * _____
_____
_____
_____

20 ___ * _____
_____
_____
_____

20 ___ * _____
_____
_____
_____

20 ___ * _____
_____
_____
_____

JANUARY

Completing one challenging task supplies the
energy to tackle another challenging task.

20 ⬭ * _____

_____

_____

20 ⬭ * _____

_____

_____

20 ⬭ * _____

_____

_____

20 ⬭ * _____

_____

_____

20 ⬭ * _____

_____

_____

_____

26 JANUARY

"It is easier to resist at the beginning than at the end."

—*Leonardo da Vinci*

20 ⬭ * _____

_____

_____

_____

20 ⬭ * _____

_____

_____

_____

20 ⬭ * _____

_____

_____

_____

20 ⬭ * _____

_____

_____

_____

20 ⬭ * _____

_____

_____

_____

JANUARY 27

When you're excited by an idea, a project seems easy,
and you move quickly. When you're not excited by an idea,
a project seems tedious, and you procrastinate.

20 ___ * _____

_____

_____

20 ___ * _____

_____

_____

20 ___ * _____

_____

_____

20 ___ * _____

_____

_____

20 ___ * _____

_____

_____

28 JANUARY

Try not to focus on having *less* or having *more*,
but on loving *what you have;* try not to focus on *doing
less* or *doing more,* but doing *what you value.*

20 __ *_____
_____
_____
_____

20 __ *_____
_____
_____
_____

20 __ *_____
_____
_____
_____

20 __ *_____
_____
_____
_____

20 __ *_____
_____
_____
_____

JANUARY 29

I sometimes feel trapped in a kind of *Groundhog Day*.
Nothing stays done; I clear a shelf, and a few weeks later,
it's covered with another mess. I replace one lightbulb,
then another bulb burns out. The same resolutions
defeat me, over and over.

20 ___ * _____

_____

_____

_____

20 ___ * _____

_____

_____

_____

20 ___ * _____

_____

_____

_____

20 ___ * _____

_____

_____

_____

20 ___ * _____

_____

_____

_____

30 JANUARY

Great souls like Samuel Johnson, Benjamin Franklin, and Saint Thérèse remade the same resolutions throughout their lives. As Johnson admitted to Boswell, "Sir, are you so grossly ignorant of human nature as not to know that a man may be very sincere in good principles, without having good practice?"

20 ___ * _____

_____

_____

_____

20 ___ * _____

_____

_____

_____

20 ___ * _____

_____

_____

_____

20 ___ * _____

_____

_____

_____

20 ___ * _____

_____

_____

_____

JANUARY

"On the whole, tho' I never arrived at the Perfection I had been so ambitious of obtaining, but fell far short of it, yet as I was, by the Endeavor, a better and a happier Man than I otherwise should have been if I had not attempted it."

—*Benjamin Franklin*

20 ___ * _____

_____

_____

_____

20 ___ * _____

_____

_____

_____

20 ___ * _____

_____

_____

_____

20 ___ * _____

_____

_____

_____

20 ___ * _____

_____

_____

_____

FEBRUARY

1

Home is where I walk through the door without ringing the bell, where I take a handful of coins from the change bowl without asking, where I eat a tuna-fish sandwich without misgivings about the ingredients, where I rifle through the mail. At the heart of my home is my family; where my family is, is home.

20 __ * _____

_____

_____

20 __ * _____

_____

_____

20 __ * _____

_____

_____

20 __ * _____

_____

_____

20 __ * _____

_____

_____

FEBRUARY

2

Behind our unremarkable front door waits the
little world of our own making, a place of safety,
exploration, comfort, and love.

20 ___ * _____

_____

_____

_____

20 ___ * _____

_____

_____

_____

20 ___ * _____

_____

_____

_____

20 ___ * _____

_____

_____

_____

20 ___ * _____

_____

_____

_____

3 FEBRUARY

At one time, messages like "Your home is a direct representation of your soul!" paralyzed me. My anxiety to do things "right" sometimes made me forget what really mattered to me. Then I realized that our home didn't have to reveal any deep truths; it's enough that it's a pleasant, comfortable place.

20 ⬤ * _____

_____

_____

_____

20 ⬤ * _____

_____

_____

_____

20 ⬤ * _____

_____

_____

_____

20 ⬤ * _____

_____

_____

_____

20 ⬤ * _____

_____

_____

_____

FEBRUARY

"Finally I am coming to the conclusion that my highest
ambition is to be what I already am."

—*Thomas Merton*

20 ___ * _____

_____

_____

_____

20 ___ * _____

_____

_____

_____

20 ___ * _____

_____

_____

_____

20 ___ * _____

_____

_____

_____

20 ___ * _____

_____

_____

_____

5 FEBRUARY

Studies suggest that we pay a price for "authenticity."
In a world so full of choices, when we choose
deliberately among alternatives, we expend mental
energy that then can't be used for other tasks.

20 ____ * _____

_____

_____

_____

20 ____ * _____

_____

_____

_____

20 ____ * _____

_____

_____

_____

20 ____ * _____

_____

_____

_____

20 ____ * _____

_____

_____

_____

FEBRUARY

Some people get tremendous creative
satisfaction from decorating their homes,
but I don't; I find it exhausting.

20 ___ * _____

_____

_____

20 ___ * _____

_____

_____

20 ___ * _____

_____

_____

20 ___ * _____

_____

_____

20 ___ * _____

_____

_____

7 FEBRUARY

When I'd first started working on the subject of happiness, I'd worried that devoting so much energy to becoming happier might be selfish or pointless. In a world so full of suffering, was it morally appropriate to seek to be happier? What was "happiness," anyway, and was it even *possible* to make myself happier?

20 ⬤ * _____
_____
_____
_____

20 ⬤ * _____
_____
_____
_____

20 ⬤ * _____
_____
_____
_____

20 ⬤ * _____
_____
_____
_____

20 ⬤ * _____
_____
_____
_____

FEBRUARY

You're not happy unless you think you're happy.

20 ⬭ * _____

_____

_____

_____

20 ⬭ * _____

_____

_____

_____

20 ⬭ * _____

_____

_____

_____

20 ⬭ * _____

_____

_____

_____

20 ⬭ * _____

_____

_____

_____

FEBRUARY

A feeling of control is a very important aspect of happiness. People who feel in control of their lives, which is powerfully bolstered by feeling in control of time, are more likely to feel happy.

20 ____ * _____

_____

_____

_____

20 ____ * _____

_____

_____

_____

20 ____ * _____

_____

_____

_____

20 ____ * _____

_____

_____

_____

20 ____ * _____

_____

_____

_____

FEBRUARY

"There is only one time that is important—
Now! It is the most important time because it is
the only time when we have any power."

—*Leo Tolstoy*

20 ___ * _____

_____

_____

20 ___ * _____

_____

_____

_____

20 ___ * _____

_____

_____

_____

20 ___ * _____

_____

_____

_____

20 ___ * _____

_____

_____

_____

11

FEBRUARY

I decided to stop making the excuse, "I don't have time to do that." I *do* have time, if I make time for the things that are important to me.

20 ⬤ * _____

_____

_____

_____

20 ⬤ * _____

_____

_____

_____

20 ⬤ * _____

_____

_____

_____

20 ⬤ * _____

_____

_____

_____

20 ⬤ * _____

_____

_____

_____

FEBRUARY 12

Instead of pursuing the impossible goal of "balance,"
seek to cram your days with the activities you love. Push
yourself to take a wider view of what is "productive."

20 ___ * _____

_____

_____

20 ___ * _____

_____

_____

20 ___ * _____

_____

_____

20 ___ * _____

_____

_____

20 ___ * _____

_____

_____

13 FEBRUARY

According to some happiness researchers, children
don't make parents happier; however, in my experience,
and I think most parents would agree, children are
indeed a significant source of happiness.

20 ___ * _____

_____

_____

_____

20 ___ * _____

_____

_____

_____

20 ___ * _____

_____

_____

_____

20 ___ * _____

_____

_____

_____

20 ___ * _____

_____

_____

_____

FEBRUARY

14

Children make us happy, in part, because they encourage
us to engage more deeply with the physical world. Their
delight in the textures and colors of Play-Doh, cotton candy,
scented markers, and velvety pipe cleaners makes us more
alive to the pleasures and experiences of daily life.

20 ___ * _____

_____

_____

20 ___ * _____

_____

_____

20 ___ * _____

_____

_____

20 ___ * _____

_____

_____

20 ___ * _____

_____

_____

15   FEBRUARY

As parents, we have great influence over not only our own
use of time but also our children's use of theirs.

20 ⬬ * _____

_____

_____

20 ⬬ * _____

_____

_____

20 ⬬ * _____

_____

_____

20 ⬬ * _____

_____

_____

20 ⬬ * _____

_____

_____

FEBRUARY 16

Many people argue that children should be required to try many different kinds of activities, to help them develop interests, but do those activities actually create new interests, where ones don't already exist? Is there a risk of squelching a budding interest, by turning it from child-chosen play into a parents' assignment?

20 ___ * _____

_____

_____

_____

20 ___ * _____

_____

_____

_____

20 ___ * _____

_____

_____

_____

20 ___ * _____

_____

_____

_____

20 ___ * _____

_____

_____

_____

17 FEBRUARY

As children or adults, when we're faced with unstructured time, with no obvious direction, no ready stimulation, and no assignments, we must choose our own occupations—a very instructive necessity.

20 ___ * _____

_____

_____

_____

20 ___ * _____

_____

_____

_____

20 ___ * _____

_____

_____

_____

20 ___ * _____

_____

_____

_____

20 ___ * _____

_____

_____

_____

FEBRUARY

18

"My mind works in idleness. To do nothing
is often my most profitable way."

— *Virginia Woolf*

20 ___ * _____

_____

_____

_____

20 ___ * _____

_____

_____

_____

20 ___ * _____

_____

_____

_____

20 ___ * _____

_____

_____

_____

20 ___ * _____

_____

_____

_____

19 FEBRUARY

Unfortunately, while it's fun and easy to *make* a resolution, it's hard to *keep* a resolution. Something like 44 percent of Americans make New Year's resolutions, but about 80 percent of resolutions are abandoned by mid-February. Many people make and break the same resolution year after year.

20 ___ * _____

_____

_____

_____

20 ___ * _____

_____

_____

_____

20 ___ * _____

_____

_____

_____

20 ___ * _____

_____

_____

_____

20 ___ * _____

_____

_____

_____

FEBRUARY

When I feel hurried and distracted, I behave worse.
I nag my husband and children more, because I want
to cross things off my list. I become too preoccupied
to notice the ordinary pleasures of my day: the colors
of the fruit at the market or my daughter's funny
stories about what happened in the lunchroom.

20 ___ * _____

_____

_____

_____

20 ___ * _____

_____

_____

_____

20 ___ * _____

_____

_____

_____

20 ___ * _____

_____

_____

_____

20 ___ * _____

_____

_____

_____

21 FEBRUARY

Feeling hurried comes in at least three flavors. With *treadmill hurry*, you feel as though you can't turn yourself off. With *to-do-list hurry*, you try to accomplish too many things in too little time. With *put-out-the-fires hurry*, you spend your time on urgent things, rather than on the things most important to you.

20 ___ * _____

_____

_____

_____

20 ___ * _____

_____

_____

_____

20 ___ * _____

_____

_____

_____

20 ___ * _____

_____

_____

_____

20 ___ * _____

_____

_____

_____

FEBRUARY 22

Many aspects of my life contributed to my feeling
of hurry. Time might seem to be a very separate issue
from possessions, for example, but I'd noticed that after
I tackled clutter, not only did our apartment seem more
spacious and organized, I also felt less hurried, because
I could find and stow things easily.

20 ___ * _____

_____

_____

_____

20 ___ * _____

_____

_____

_____

20 ___ * _____

_____

_____

_____

20 ___ * _____

_____

_____

_____

20 ___ * _____

_____

_____

_____

23 FEBRUARY

Within the larger subject of happiness, the proper relationship of possessions to happiness is hotly debated. People often argue that possessions don't—or shouldn't— matter much to happiness, but I think they do.

20___ * _____

_____

_____

_____

20___ * _____

_____

_____

_____

20___ * _____

_____

_____

_____

20___ * _____

_____

_____

_____

20___ * _____

_____

_____

_____

FEBRUARY

As you're clearing clutter in your home, work through a quick checklist: Do we use it? Do we love it? You'll recognize the important difference between something that *wasn't used* and something that was *useless*.

20 ___ * _____

_____

_____

20 ___ * _____

_____

_____

20 ___ * _____

_____

_____

20 ___ * _____

_____

_____

20 ___ * _____

_____

_____

25 FEBRUARY

"Have nothing in your houses that you do not know
to be useful, or believe to be beautiful."

—*William Morris*

20 ___ * _____

_____

_____

_____

20 ___ * _____

_____

_____

_____

20 ___ * _____

_____

_____

_____

20 ___ * _____

_____

_____

_____

20 ___ * _____

_____

_____

_____

FEBRUARY 26

Happiness is not having *less;* happiness is not
having *more;* happiness is wanting *what you have.*
And this truth has an important corollary: If you don't
want something, getting it won't make you happy.

20 ___ * _____

_____

_____

20 ___ * _____

_____

_____

20 ___ * _____

_____

_____

20 ___ * _____

_____

_____

20 ___ * _____

_____

_____

_____

27 FEBRUARY

Attachment brings happiness, and attachment brings unhappiness. Love—for people, for possessions, for a place, for an animal, for a house, for anything—exposes us to the pain of loss. It's inescapable. We can mitigate that pain by moderating or even eliminating attachment, but while something is gained, something is also relinquished.

20 ___ * _____

_____

_____

_____

20 ___ * _____

_____

_____

_____

20 ___ * _____

_____

_____

_____

20 ___ * _____

_____

_____

_____

20 ___ * _____

_____

_____

_____

FEBRUARY 28

"We need to project ourselves into the things around us.
My self is not confined to my body. It extends into all
the things I have made and all the things around me.
Without these things, I would not be myself."

—Carl Jung

20 ___ *_____
_____
_____
_____

20 ___ *_____
_____
_____
_____

20 ___ *_____
_____
_____
_____

20 ___ *_____
_____
_____
_____

20 ___ *_____
_____
_____
_____

29   **FEBRUARY**

Every day, whenever the thought occurs to me,
I do some kind of jump. I jump in a silly way to make
my daughters laugh, I give a little secret skip on my
way to the drugstore, I do jumping jacks after I wake
up in the morning. The sheer goofiness of it always
makes me feel cheerier and more energetic.

20 ⬭ * _____

_____

_____

_____

20 ⬭ * _____

_____

_____

_____

20 ⬭ * _____

_____

_____

_____

20 ⬭ * _____

_____

_____

_____

20 ⬭ * _____

_____

_____

_____

MARCH

If I want to feel cheerful, energetic, and mentally sharp,
I *have* to get enough sleep—even if that means leaving
e-mails unread or putting down a book in midchapter.

20 ___ * _____

_____

_____

20 ___ * _____

_____

_____

20 ___ * _____

_____

_____

20 ___ * _____

_____

_____

20 ___ * _____

_____

_____

_____

2 MARCH

I don't check e-mail at bedtime. I love ending the day
with an emptier in-box, but the stimulation of reading
e-mails wakes me right up, and as a consequence, I often
have trouble falling asleep. Unless someone is crying,
throwing up, or smells smoke, sleep is my first priority.

20 ⬤ * _____

_____

_____

_____

20 ⬤ * _____

_____

_____

_____

20 ⬤ * _____

_____

_____

_____

20 ⬤ * _____

_____

_____

_____

20 ⬤ * _____

_____

_____

_____

MARCH

"Goodnight stars. Goodnight air.
Goodnight noises everywhere."

—*Margaret Wise Brown,* **Goodnight Moon**

20 ___ * _____

_____

_____

20 ___ * _____

_____

_____

20 ___ * _____

_____

_____

20 ___ * _____

_____

_____

20 ___ * _____

_____

_____

MARCH

I'm lucky: I love my work, and I look forward to working. But my feeling that I should be working, or my choice to work instead of to do other things that are also important sometimes interferes with my long-term happiness.

20 ___ * _____

_____

_____

_____

20 ___ * _____

_____

_____

_____

20 ___ * _____

_____

_____

_____

20 ___ * _____

_____

_____

_____

20 ___ * _____

_____

_____

_____

MARCH

5

Technology has created new kinds of work that seem to demand constant, immediate attention. *I should answer my e-mails. I should look at that link. I should check Facebook and Twitter.*

20 ___ * _____

_____

_____

_____

20 ___ * _____

_____

_____

_____

20 ___ * _____

_____

_____

_____

20 ___ * _____

_____

_____

_____

20 ___ * _____

_____

_____

_____

6

MARCH

Technology is a good servant but a bad master. What's more, online tasks give you an easy way to be fake-productive. Working is one of the most dangerous forms of procrastination.

20 ⬤ * _____

_____

_____

_____

20 ⬤ * _____

_____

_____

_____

20 ⬤ * _____

_____

_____

_____

20 ⬤ * _____

_____

_____

_____

20 ⬤ * _____

_____

_____

_____

MARCH

"When I think about what sort of person I would most like to have on a retainer, I think it would be a boss. A boss who could tell me what to do, because that makes everything easy when you're working."

— *Andy Warhol*

20 ___ * _____

_____

_____

_____

20 ___ * _____

_____

_____

_____

20 ___ * _____

_____

_____

_____

20 ___ * _____

_____

_____

_____

20 ___ * _____

_____

_____

_____

MARCH

I know I shouldn't really blame technology.
The real problem isn't the switch on my computer,
but the switch inside my mind. To be more focused,
I must control the cubicle in my pocket.

20 ___ * _____

_____

_____

_____

20 ___ * _____

_____

_____

_____

20 ___ * _____

_____

_____

_____

20 ___ * _____

_____

_____

_____

20 ___ * _____

_____

_____

_____

MARCH

I don't check my e-mail or talk on the phone when I'm traveling from one place to another, whether by foot, bus, subway, or taxi. I've realized that many of my most important ideas have come to me during these times.

20 ___ * _____

_____

_____

_____

20 ___ * _____

_____

_____

_____

20 ___ * _____

_____

_____

_____

20 ___ * _____

_____

_____

_____

20 ___ * _____

_____

_____

_____

10 MARCH

Whenever you can, mute your cell phone.
Someone coined the term "fauxcellarm" to
describe the jumpy feeling you get when you
imagine that your cell phone is ringing.

20 ___ * _____

_____

_____

_____

20 ___ * _____

_____

_____

_____

20 ___ * _____

_____

_____

_____

20 ___ * _____

_____

_____

_____

20 ___ * _____

_____

_____

_____

MARCH

Embrace the fact that you may do a lot
of connecting with friends and acquaintances
through technology. Although nothing replaces
face-to-face meetings, it is better to use those
tools than not to connect at all.

20 ___ * _____

_____

_____

20 ___ * _____

_____

_____

20 ___ * _____

_____

_____

20 ___ * _____

_____

_____

20 ___ * _____

_____

_____

12 MARCH

One of the most important aspects of home is the celebration of traditions. Family traditions mark time in a happy way and give a sense both of anticipation and continuity. Research shows that traditions, routines, and rituals boost physical and emotional health. And they're *fun*.

20 ___ * _____

20 ___ * _____

20 ___ * _____

20 ___ * _____

20 ___ * _____

MARCH 13

I love traditions—but I dislike hassle. I can barely
keep up with the big traditions we already celebrate
(not to mention the demands of ordinary life). So I
looked for a way to incorporate more of the fun of
traditions, in a way that was meaningful yet painless.
I wanted to keep it simple, but not *too* simple.

20 ___ * _____

_____

_____

20 ___ * _____

_____

_____

20 ___ * _____

_____

_____

20 ___ * _____

_____

_____

20 ___ * _____

_____

_____

14 MARCH

I made a note on my calendar for the week of March 14:
"Remember decorations for St. Patrick's Day breakfast."
School-day breakfasts blur and disappear, but little celebrations make some days stand out. For someone like me,
it is gratifying to celebrate minor holidays in a very manageable way. I can choose the bigger life, by thinking smaller.

20 ⬤ * _____

_____

_____

_____

20 ⬤ * _____

_____

_____

_____

20 ⬤ * _____

_____

_____

_____

20 ⬤ * _____

_____

_____

_____

20 ⬤ * _____

_____

_____

_____

MARCH 15

Gratitude is a key to a happy life. People who cultivate gratitude get a boost in happiness and optimism, feel more connected to others, are better liked, have more friends, and are more likely to help others—they even sleep better and have fewer headaches. Grateful feelings crowd out negative emotions like anger, envy, and resentment.

20 ___ * _____

_____

_____

_____

20 ___ * _____

_____

_____

_____

20 ___ * _____

_____

_____

_____

20 ___ * _____

_____

_____

_____

20 ___ * _____

_____

_____

_____

16 MARCH

I had an opportunity for gratitude on March 16, the night before St. Patrick's Day. I was exhausted, and I really didn't feel like setting the table for a holiday breakfast—but I'd made the resolution to "Celebrate holiday breakfasts." I admonished myself, "I'm so *grateful* to have two girls who are still young enough to be excited by a green breakfast!"

20 ___ * _____

_____

_____

_____

20 ___ * _____

_____

_____

_____

20 ___ * _____

_____

_____

_____

20 ___ * _____

_____

_____

_____

20 ___ * _____

_____

_____

_____

MARCH 17

"Don't let the perfect be the enemy of the good."

— *Voltaire*

20 ___ * _____

_____

_____

20 ___ * _____

_____

_____

20 ___ * _____

_____

_____

20 ___ * _____

_____

_____

20 ___ * _____

_____

_____

_____

18 MARCH

"Live as long as you may, the first twenty years are the longest half of your life. They appear so while they are passing; they seem to have been so when we look back on them; and they take up more room in our memory than all the years that succeed them."

—*Robert Southey*

20 ⬭ * _____

_____

_____

_____

20 ⬭ * _____

_____

_____

_____

20 ⬭ * _____

_____

_____

_____

20 ⬭ * _____

_____

_____

_____

20 ⬭ * _____

_____

_____

_____

MARCH 19

The days are long, but the years are short, and I know
that this time that seems so long—my husband and I,
with our girls, all under the same roof—will actually
be just a short period over the course of my life. I want
to notice the quality of this time and appreciate it.

20 ___ * _____

_____

_____

20 ___ * _____

_____

_____

20 ___ * _____

_____

_____

20 ___ * _____

_____

_____

20 ___ * _____

_____

_____

20   MARCH

Although I want a sense of thankfulness to permeate
the atmosphere of my home, I find it challenging to
cultivate gratitude. It is too easy to fail to appreciate
all the things I'm grateful for—from pervasive, basic things
like running water, to major, personal aspects of my life
such as the fact that my family is in good health.

20 _____ * _____

_____

_____

_____

20 _____ * _____

_____

_____

_____

20 _____ * _____

_____

_____

_____

20 _____ * _____

_____

_____

_____

20 _____ * _____

_____

_____

_____

MARCH 21

To remind myself to feel grateful for everything I have,
and for my dear ordinary life, I've decided to "follow a
threshold ritual." Each time I stand at the top of the steps to
my building, I repeat, "How happy I am, how grateful I am,
to be home." Every time I cross the threshold from the
street, I take a moment to reflect lovingly on my family.

20 ___ * _____

_____

_____

_____

20 ___ * _____

_____

_____

_____

20 ___ * _____

_____

_____

_____

20 ___ * _____

_____

_____

_____

20 ___ * _____

_____

_____

_____

22 MARCH

"'Safe! safe! safe!' the pulse of the house beats wildly. Waking, I cry 'Oh, is this *your* buried treasure? The light in the heart.'"

— *Virginia Woolf*

20 ⬤ * _____

_____

_____

20 ⬤ * _____

_____

_____

20 ⬤ * _____

_____

_____

20 ⬤ * _____

_____

_____

20 ⬤ * _____

_____

_____

MARCH 23

At night, if I can't sleep, I walk from room to
room in our apartment to look at the sleeping faces
of my family—safe, safe, safe—then I stand by the
window in the dark and gaze across the street to
the dark buildings there. I'm always cheered to see
a few glowing lights, signs of neighbors nearby.

20 ___ * _____

_____

_____

_____

20 ___ * _____

_____

_____

_____

20 ___ * _____

_____

_____

_____

20 ___ * _____

_____

_____

_____

20 ___ * _____

_____

_____

_____

24 MARCH

At the neighborhood library where I often work,
or at the various coffee shops I haunt, I have a delicious
feeling of solitude and absorption, because it's not *being
alone* that matters; it's not being *interrupted*.

20 ⬭ * _____

_____

_____

_____

20 ⬭ * _____

_____

_____

_____

20 ⬭ * _____

_____

_____

_____

20 ⬭ * _____

_____

_____

_____

20 ⬭ * _____

_____

_____

_____

MARCH

25

Research suggests that a person may need at least
fifteen minutes to regain focus after even a quick break
in concentration, and when people are interrupted, they
work faster to make up for lost time, and this hurrying
makes them feel frustrated and harried.

20 ___ * _____

_____

_____

_____

20 ___ * _____

_____

_____

_____

20 ___ * _____

_____

_____

_____

20 ___ * _____

_____

_____

_____

20 ___ * _____

_____

_____

_____

26 MARCH

I'd been snapping at my daughters when they came into my office, when finally I asked myself, "What's the problem? I *like* to have them come to my office. I just react badly when they break my focus." And suddenly I saw the solution. The girls should *knock*! Somehow, that act of courtesy allowed me to change the way I answered.

20 ___ * _____

_____

_____

_____

20 ___ * _____

_____

_____

_____

20 ___ * _____

_____

_____

_____

20 ___ * _____

_____

_____

_____

20 ___ * _____

_____

_____

_____

MARCH

"Life is not so short but that there is
always time for courtesy."

—*Ralph Waldo Emerson*

20 ___ * _____

_____

_____

_____

20 ___ * _____

_____

_____

_____

20 ___ * _____

_____

_____

_____

20 ___ * _____

_____

_____

_____

20 ___ * _____

_____

_____

_____

28 MARCH

Relationship expert John Gottman emphasizes the importance of responding to "bids"; when someone makes an attempt to connect with a touch, question, gesture, comment, or look, we should answer with a comment, a laugh, or some kind of acknowledgement.

20 ___ * _____

_____

_____

_____

20 ___ * _____

_____

_____

_____

20 ___ * _____

_____

_____

_____

20 ___ * _____

_____

_____

_____

20 ___ * _____

_____

_____

_____

MARCH 29

As I started to focus on the issue of my husband's response to my bids for his attention, I had to admit that *I* could do a much better job of acknowledging *his* bids. Murmuring "Mmhh, mmhh . . ." with my eyes glued to a book wasn't the way to foster intimacy and affection.

20 __ *_____

_____

_____

20 __ *_____

_____

_____

20 __ *_____

_____

_____

20 __ *_____

_____

_____

20 __ *_____

_____

_____

30 MARCH

Act the way you want to feel. By acting in a thoughtful, loving way, I boosted my feelings of tenderness toward my family. And that contributed more to the happiness of our home than anything else I could do.

20 ___ * _____

_____

_____

_____

20 ___ * _____

_____

_____

_____

20 ___ * _____

_____

_____

_____

20 ___ * _____

_____

_____

_____

20 ___ * _____

_____

_____

_____

MARCH

"Such as are your habitual thoughts,
such also will be the character of your mind;
for the soul is dyed by the thoughts."

— *Marcus Aurelius*

20 ___ * _____

_____

_____

20 ___ * _____

_____

_____

20 ___ * _____

_____

_____

20 ___ * _____

_____

_____

20 ___ * _____

_____

_____

1

APRIL

"Anything one does every day is
important and imposing and anywhere
one lives is interesting and beautiful."

—*Gertrude Stein*

20 ___ * _____

_____

_____

_____

20 ___ * _____

_____

_____

_____

20 ___ * _____

_____

_____

_____

20 ___ * _____

_____

_____

_____

20 ___ * _____

_____

_____

_____

APRIL

April, with its warmer weather, was a good month
to think about my neighborhood, because I no longer
had to rush from door to door to avoid the cold. My more
leisurely daily walks heightened my desire to engage
with the places and people around me.

20 ___ * _____

_____

_____

20 ___ * _____

_____

_____

20 ___ * _____

_____

_____

20 ___ * _____

_____

_____

20 ___ * _____

_____

_____

_____

3 APRIL

Research shows that people who remind themselves
of the excellence and beauty in their lives have a greater
sense of meaning and happiness. Try to combine the
pleasures of being at home and on holiday, by making
an effort to see the familiar with new eyes.

20 ___ * _____
_____
_____
_____

20 ___ * _____
_____
_____
_____

20 ___ * _____
_____
_____
_____

20 ___ * _____
_____
_____
_____

20 ___ * _____
_____
_____
_____

APRIL

"I love a broad margin to my life."

—*Thoreau*

20 ___ * _____

_____

_____

_____

20 ___ * _____

_____

_____

_____

20 ___ * _____

_____

_____

_____

20 ___ * _____

_____

_____

_____

20 ___ * _____

_____

_____

_____

5 APRIL

Historian Mircea Eliade describes the "privileged places" of our lives, which might include "a man's birthplace, or the scenes of his first love, or certain places in the first foreign city he visited in youth." We all have our own private landmarks, our personal historical sites, our favorite corners.

20____ * _____

_____

_____

_____

20____ * _____

_____

_____

_____

20____ * _____

_____

_____

_____

20____ * _____

_____

_____

_____

20____ * _____

_____

_____

_____

APRIL

Call up past memories. As you travel the streets each day, make an effort to recall important memories connected to the places you visit.

20 ___ * _____
_____
_____
_____

20 ___ * _____
_____
_____
_____

20 ___ * _____
_____
_____
_____

20 ___ * _____
_____
_____
_____

20 ___ * _____
_____
_____
_____

7

APRIL

Be a tourist without leaving home. "Be a tourist" doesn't mean visiting every tourist spot in your area. It means having the eye and the enthusiasm of a tourist: a tourist reads and studies, a tourist shows up, a tourist sees things with fresh eyes.

20 ___ * _____

_____

_____

_____

20 ___ * _____

_____

_____

_____

20 ___ * _____

_____

_____

_____

20 ___ * _____

_____

_____

_____

20 ___ * _____

_____

_____

_____

APRIL

8

> "The true secret of happiness *lies in the taking a genuine interest in all the details of daily life.*"
>
> —*William Morris*

20 ___ * _____

_____

_____

_____

20 ___ * _____

_____

_____

_____

20 ___ * _____

_____

_____

_____

20 ___ * _____

_____

_____

_____

20 ___ * _____

_____

_____

_____

APRIL

Learn more. I wanted to learn more about the place where I live. Whenever I visited a foreign city, I read a guidebook, and so I read guidebooks for New York City. We'd owned a copy of Kenneth Jackson's enormous *Encyclopedia of New York City* for years; I moved it from a high shelf to the coffee table, and browsed whenever I had a minute.

20 ___ * _____

_____

_____

_____

20 ___ * _____

_____

_____

_____

20 ___ * _____

_____

_____

_____

20 ___ * _____

_____

_____

_____

20 ___ * _____

_____

_____

_____

APRIL 10

Being a tourist is a state of mind.

20 ___ * _____

_____

_____

_____

20 ___ * _____

_____

_____

_____

20 ___ * _____

_____

_____

_____

20 ___ * _____

_____

_____

_____

20 ___ * _____

_____

_____

_____

11 APRIL

Choose the bigger life.

20 ___ * _____
_____
_____
_____

20 ___ * _____
_____
_____
_____

20 ___ * _____
_____
_____
_____

20 ___ * _____
_____
_____
_____

20 ___ * _____
_____
_____
_____

APRIL 12

"My favorite thing is to go where I've never been before."

—*Diane Arbus*

20 ___ * _____

_____

_____

20 ___ * _____

_____

_____

20 ___ * _____

_____

_____

20 ___ * _____

_____

_____

20 ___ * _____

_____

_____

13 APRIL

I tried to identify ways to do more nonrandom acts
of kindness, and to make people happier in my presence,
on a very small scale. First of all, I aimed to do a better
job with simple politeness (the lowest level of kindness,
but nevertheless important). I also made more effort
to notice when other people needed a hand.

20 _____ * _____

_____

_____

_____

20 _____ * _____

_____

_____

_____

20 _____ * _____

_____

_____

_____

20 _____ * _____

_____

_____

_____

20 _____ * _____

_____

_____

_____

APRIL

14

"Good manners are made up of petty sacrifices."

—*Ralph Waldo Emerson*

20 ___ * _____

20 ___ * _____

20 ___ * _____

20 ___ * _____

20 ___ * _____

15   APRIL

Of all the elements that make up a neighborhood,
the most important are the neighbors, and I wanted to
act with greater neighborliness, to work harder to add
to the happiness of the people I encountered in my day,
in my building, or during my usual routine.

20 ___ * _____

_____

_____

_____

20 ___ * _____

_____

_____

_____

20 ___ * _____

_____

_____

_____

20 ___ * _____

_____

_____

_____

20 ___ * _____

_____

_____

APRIL 16

I ask myself, does my presence make people happier?

20___ * _____
_____
_____
_____

20___ * _____
_____
_____
_____

20___ * _____
_____
_____
_____

20___ * _____
_____
_____
_____

20___ * _____
_____
_____
_____

17 APRIL

I wish I were more open and outgoing, but I'm not. What nonrandom act of kindness could I do within the confines of my own nature? I decided to make a much bigger effort to bring people together—such as inviting newcomers to join my various reading and writing groups— and in particular, to recommend people for work.

20 ___ * _____

_____

_____

_____

20 ___ * _____

_____

_____

_____

20 ___ * _____

_____

_____

_____

20 ___ * _____

_____

_____

_____

20 ___ * _____

_____

_____

_____

APRIL

18

"'You must be a friend,' said Corduroy.
'I've always wanted a friend.'

'Me too!' said Lisa, and gave him a big hug."

—*Don Freeman,* **Corduroy**

20 ___ * _____

_____

_____

_____

20 ___ * _____

_____

_____

_____

20 ___ * _____

_____

_____

_____

20 ___ * _____

_____

_____

_____

20 ___ * _____

_____

_____

_____

19 APRIL

Every time I step through the doorway to my apartment,
I'm hit by the particular sense of *home* created by
everything from the scents I encounter, to the way I'm
greeted by my family, to the level of mess I confront.

20 ⬭ *_____

_____

_____

_____

20 ⬭ *_____

_____

_____

_____

20 ⬭ *_____

_____

_____

_____

20 ⬭ *_____

_____

_____

_____

20 ⬭ *_____

_____

_____

_____

APRIL

Because happiness can seem very abstract and
transcendent, focusing on my body is a way to keep
my resolutions specific and tangible; also, things that
I experience physically hold a special power.

20 ___ * _____

_____

_____

_____

20 ___ * _____

_____

_____

_____

20 ___ * _____

_____

_____

_____

20 ___ * _____

_____

_____

_____

20 ___ * _____

_____

_____

_____

21 APRIL

The more I think about happiness, the more convinced I become of the value of the concrete. Airy recommendations like "Find ways to bounce back," "Love yourself," or "Be optimistic" strike me as unhelpfully vague. I find it easier to follow resolutions that can clearly be evaluated, such as "Sing in the morning" or "Keep a one-sentence journal."

20 ___ * _____

_____

_____

_____

20 ___ * _____

_____

_____

_____

20 ___ * _____

_____

_____

_____

20 ___ * _____

_____

_____

_____

20 ___ * _____

_____

_____

_____

APRIL 22

"Let us decide on the route that we wish to take to pass our life, and attempt to sow that route with flowers."

—Madame du Chatelet

20 ___ * _____

20 ___ * _____

20 ___ * _____

20 ___ * _____

20 ___ * _____

23

APRIL

Experience the experience.

20 ___ * _____

_____

_____

_____

20 ___ * _____

_____

_____

_____

20 ___ * _____

_____

_____

_____

20 ___ * _____

_____

_____

_____

20 ___ * _____

_____

_____

_____

APRIL 24

I use scent as a cue to experience the experience—to be alive to the present moment, and to my memories. I love the smell of popcorn, which makes me think of my mother, and the smell of crayons, which make me think of childhood. How I wish I could smell again the baked, woody, spicy fragrance of the attic of my parents' old house.

20 ___ * _____

_____

_____

_____

20 ___ * _____

_____

_____

_____

20 ___ * _____

_____

_____

_____

20 ___ * _____

_____

_____

_____

20 ___ * _____

_____

_____

_____

25 APRIL

Few pleasures have the simplicity of a lovely scent;
it doesn't cost anything, doesn't require anyone
else's cooperation, doesn't have any calories,
and doesn't take any planning or time to enjoy.
It's a quick hit of an innocent indulgence.

20 ⬭ * _____

_____

_____

20 ⬭ * _____

_____

_____

20 ⬭ * _____

_____

_____

20 ⬭ * _____

_____

_____

20 ⬭ * _____

_____

_____

APRIL 26

How else to add good smells to my life? I prompted myself to pay attention when I covered my daughter with baby lotion, which is one of my very favorite smells. In the middle of winter, I couldn't stop to smell the roses, but I could take a moment to bury my face in a pile of towels, to enjoy that hot, clean fragrance as they came from the dryer.

20 ____ * _____
_____
_____
_____

20 ____ * _____
_____
_____
_____

20 ____ * _____
_____
_____
_____

20 ____ * _____
_____
_____
_____

20 ____ * _____
_____
_____
_____

27 APRIL

Manual occupations like gardening, woodworking, cooking, doing home repairs, caring for pets, working on a car, or knitting can be deeply satisfying on many levels: the physical motion, the tangibility of the accomplishments, the pleasure of the tools, the sensory delights of the materials.

20 ___ * _____

_____

_____

_____

20 ___ * _____

_____

_____

_____

20 ___ * _____

_____

_____

_____

20 ___ * _____

_____

_____

_____

20 ___ * _____

_____

_____

_____

APRIL

28

Even activities that are clearly highly creative—editing a video or designing a website—don't offer the same kind of tactile gratification as activities done by hand, while activities so simple they hardly qualify as "creative"—building a fire or organizing a drawer—are deeply satisfying in this concrete way.

20 ___ * _____

_____

_____

20 ___ * _____

_____

_____

20 ___ * _____

_____

_____

20 ___ * _____

_____

_____

20 ___ * _____

_____

_____

29 APRIL

A familiar and influential line of argument is that happiness isn't a goal that can be directly pursued, but rather is the indirect consequence of a life well lived. Eleanor Roosevelt summed this up: "Happiness is not a goal; it is a by-product." But that's a false choice.

20 ___ * _____

20 ___ * _____

20 ___ * _____

20 ___ * _____

20 ___ * _____

APRIL

In the area of happiness, false choices seem particularly alluring. Instead of facing an intimidating array of options, we face a few simple possibilities (i.e.: "I can have a few close friends, or a bunch of superficial relationships"). But although false choices can be comforting, they can leave us feeling trapped and blinded to other alternatives.

20 ____ * _____

_____

_____

_____

20 ____ * _____

_____

_____

_____

20 ____ * _____

_____

_____

_____

20 ____ * _____

_____

_____

20 ____ * _____

_____

_____

_____

1

MAY

Happiness is a goal *and* a by-product.
The activities a person would undertake to pursue
happiness directly are identical to the activities
that would yield happiness indirectly.

20 ___ * _____

_____

_____

_____

20 ___ * _____

_____

_____

_____

20 ___ * _____

_____

_____

_____

20 ___ * _____

_____

_____

_____

20 ___ * _____

_____

_____

_____

MAY

2

We're more likely to hit a target by aiming at it than by ignoring it, and happiness is no different.

20 ___ * _____

_____

_____

20 ___ * _____

_____

_____

20 ___ * _____

_____

_____

20 ___ * _____

_____

_____

20 ___ * _____

_____

_____

_____

3   **MAY**

"Where Thou art—that—is Home—"

—*Emily Dickinson*

20 ⬤ * _____

_____

_____

_____

20 ⬤ * _____

_____

_____

_____

20 ⬤ * _____

_____

_____

_____

20 ⬤ * _____

_____

_____

_____

20 ⬤ * _____

_____

_____

_____

MAY

Married people are so intertwined, so interdependent, so symbiotic, that it's hard to maintain a sense of wonder and excitement. I love my husband passionately, but he pervades my entire life, so now sometimes it's hard to see him.

20 ___ * _____

_____

_____

_____

20 ___ * _____

_____

_____

_____

20 ___ * _____

_____

_____

_____

20 ___ * _____

_____

_____

_____

20 ___ * _____

_____

_____

_____

5 MAY

Although I'm sometimes tempted to hand my husband a long list of all the (to my mind, quite reasonable) changes he should make to boost my happiness, the fact is, I can write that list only for myself. Nevertheless, when I change, our relationship changes, and my husband changes.

20 ___ * _____

_____

_____

_____

20 ___ * _____

_____

_____

_____

20 ___ * _____

_____

_____

_____

20 ___ * _____

_____

_____

_____

20 ___ * _____

_____

_____

_____

MAY

"It is difficult to bring people to goodness with lessons,
but it is easy to do so by example."

— *Seneca*

20 __ * _____

_____

_____

_____

20 __ * _____

_____

_____

_____

20 __ * _____

_____

_____

_____

20 __ * _____

_____

_____

_____

20 __ * _____

_____

_____

_____

7

MAY

If I've learned one thing from my happiness project,
it's that if I want my life to be a certain way, *I* must
be that way myself. If I want my marriage to be tender
and romantic, *I* must be tender and romantic.

20 ___ * _____

_____

_____

_____

20 ___ * _____

_____

_____

_____

20 ___ * _____

_____

_____

_____

20 ___ * _____

_____

_____

_____

20 ___ * _____

_____

_____

_____

MAY

I want to be emotionally self-sufficient, so I don't depend on other people or circumstances to boost me up, and don't let them drag me down. When I feel unhappy, it becomes too easy to suck happy energy from others; or to demand constant praise, affirmation, or reassurance.

20 ___ * _____

_____

_____

_____

20 ___ * _____

_____

_____

_____

20 ___ * _____

_____

_____

_____

20 ___ * _____

_____

_____

_____

20 ___ * _____

_____

_____

_____

MAY

While I aim for my own built-in happiness, I know that relationships matter tremendously for my happiness. Because of the psychological phenomenon of "emotional contagion," we "catch" emotions from other people.

20 ___ * _____

_____

_____

_____

20 ___ * _____

_____

_____

_____

20 ___ * _____

_____

_____

_____

20 ___ * _____

_____

_____

_____

20 ___ * _____

_____

_____

_____

MAY

Cheerfulness is contagious, and crabbiness
is even more contagious.

20 ⬤ * _____

_____

_____

_____

20 ⬤ * _____

_____

_____

_____

20 ⬤ * _____

_____

_____

_____

20 ⬤ * _____

_____

_____

_____

20 ⬤ * _____

_____

_____

_____

11   **MAY**

I want my husband and children to be happy,
but I can't *make* them be happy, and I don't want
to take my happiness entirely from them.

20 ___ * _____

_____

_____

_____

20 ___ * _____

_____

_____

_____

20 ___ * _____

_____

_____

_____

20 ___ * _____

_____

_____

_____

20 ___ * _____

_____

_____

_____

MAY

12

"The habit of being happy enables one to be freed, or largely freed, from the dominance of the outward conditions."

—*Robert Louis Stevenson*

20 ___ *_____

_____

_____

_____

20 ___ *_____

_____

_____

_____

20 ___ *_____

_____

_____

_____

20 ___ *_____

_____

_____

_____

20 ___ *_____

_____

_____

_____

13   MAY

"To hear complaints is wearisome alike
to the wretched and the happy."

— *Samuel Johnson*

20 ⬤ * _____

_____

_____

_____

20 ⬤ * _____

_____

_____

_____

20 ⬤ * _____

_____

_____

_____

20 ⬤ * _____

_____

_____

_____

20 ⬤ * _____

_____

_____

_____

MAY

14

Studies show that married people actually treat each other with less civility than they show to other people. Whether while talking casually or working on a task, people were less courteous and tactful with a spouse than with a person they didn't know well.

20 ___ * _____

_____

_____

_____

20 ___ * _____

_____

_____

_____

20 ___ * _____

_____

_____

_____

20 ___ * _____

_____

_____

_____

20 ___ * _____

_____

_____

_____

15

MAY

Couples who don't tolerate much bad behavior
from each other at the beginning of a relationship
are happier in that relationship later.

20 ____ * _____

_____

_____

_____

20 ____ * _____

_____

_____

_____

20 ____ * _____

_____

_____

_____

20 ____ * _____

_____

_____

_____

20 ____ * _____

_____

_____

_____

MAY 16

My home is a reflection of me: it would be serene, festive,
loving, and welcoming only if I brought that spirit to it.
To feel more at home at home, I must carry my home,
my treasure, within me. A happy home isn't a place that I
could furnish, but an attitude of mind I must develop.

20 ___ * _____

_____

_____

_____

20 ___ * _____

_____

_____

_____

20 ___ * _____

_____

_____

_____

20 ___ * _____

_____

_____

_____

20 ___ * _____

_____

_____

_____

17

MAY

Each period of life has its own atmosphere, its own flavor. My husband and I are in the thick of middle marriage: children at home, midcareer, homeownership, milestone birthdays. I want to do more to appreciate this stage of life and make sure this time doesn't slip away unremarked.

20 ⬭ __ * _____

_____

_____

_____

20 ⬭ __ * _____

_____

_____

_____

20 ⬭ __ * _____

_____

_____

_____

20 ⬭ __ * _____

_____

_____

_____

20 ⬭ __ * _____

_____

_____

_____

MAY 18

"One lives in the naïve notion that *later* there
will be more room than in the entire past."

—*Elias Canetti*

20 ___ * _____

_____

_____

_____

20 ___ * _____

_____

_____

_____

20 ___ * _____

_____

_____

_____

20 ___ * _____

_____

_____

_____

20 ___ * _____

_____

_____

_____

19 MAY

I'm a big believer in the importance of family photos. Recalling happy memories from the past gives a boost to happiness in the present, and looking at photographs of beloved people is an easy way to engineer a mood boost.

20 ___ * _____

_____

_____

_____

20 ___ * _____

_____

_____

_____

20 ___ * _____

_____

_____

_____

20 ___ * _____

_____

_____

_____

20 ___ * _____

_____

_____

MAY

Casual snapshots are as important as formal family portraits. I would never have imagined that I could forget my daughter's excitement in showing off her newly pierced ears, yet when I caught sight of a photo of this milestone moment, I realized with alarm that my memories had already started to fade.

20 __ * _____

_____

_____

20 __ * _____

_____

_____

20 __ * _____

_____

_____

20 __ * _____

_____

_____

20 __ * _____

_____

_____

_____

21 MAY

"This is the most exciting night of my life!" my daughter said, shaking with exhilaration. "My *tooth* is *loose*!" Her excitement, her high piping voice, that very first tooth; I wanted never to forget this.

20 ⬭ __ * _____

_____

_____

_____

20 ⬭ __ * _____

_____

_____

_____

20 ⬭ __ * _____

_____

_____

_____

20 ⬭ __ * _____

_____

_____

_____

20 ⬭ __ * _____

_____

_____

_____

MAY

22

"'What kind of story would you like to hear?' said Mother Bear.

'Tell me about me,' said Little Bear. 'Tell me about the things I once did.'"

—*Else Holmelund Minarik, **Little Bear***

20 ___ * _____

_____

_____

_____

20 ___ * _____

_____

_____

_____

20 ___ * _____

_____

_____

_____

20 ___ * _____

_____

_____

_____

20 ___ * _____

_____

_____

_____

23

MAY

Often when I have an idea for a creative undertaking, it seems straightforward and fun, but as I get deeper in, I realize how much time, energy, and effort will be required to carry through. It's hard to do even simple things well, and most things aren't simple.

20 ___ * _____

_____

_____

_____

20 ___ * _____

_____

_____

_____

20 ___ * _____

_____

_____

_____

20 ___ * _____

_____

_____

_____

20 ___ * _____

_____

_____

_____

MAY

24

When my sister and I decided to collaborate on a project, I wondered if even my small contribution would be too great a responsibility and distraction. Maybe I should focus my energies on my own work? Keep it simple. No! *Bigger.* I have plenty of time to do the things that are important to me.

20 ___ * _____

_____

_____

_____

20 ___ * _____

_____

_____

_____

20 ___ * _____

_____

_____

_____

20 ___ * _____

_____

_____

_____

20 ___ * _____

_____

_____

_____

25 MAY

I'd expected to enjoy collaborating with my sister, and I certainly did, but I also found that just *talking* to her more often made a big difference. Now that we had a particular reason to call, we talked more, and, no surprise, I felt closer to her.

20 ___ * _____

_____

_____

_____

20 ___ * _____

_____

_____

_____

20 ___ * _____

_____

_____

_____

20 ___ * _____

_____

_____

_____

20 ___ * _____

_____

_____

_____

MAY

Pouring out ideas is better for creativity than
doling them out by the teaspoon.

20 ___ * _____

_____

_____

_____

20 ___ * _____

_____

_____

_____

20 ___ * _____

_____

_____

_____

20 ___ * _____

_____

_____

_____

20 ___ * _____

_____

_____

_____

27 MAY

"One does not play Bach without having done scales. But neither does one play a scale merely for the sake of the scale."

—Simone Weil

20 ⬭ * _____

_____

_____

_____

20 ⬭ * _____

_____

_____

_____

20 ⬭ * _____

_____

_____

_____

20 ⬭ * _____

_____

_____

_____

20 ⬭ * _____

_____

_____

_____

MAY

28

The feeling of growth and movement toward a goal is very important to happiness—just as important, and perhaps more important, than finally reaching that goal. Nietzsche captured this tension: "The end of a melody is not its goal; but nonetheless, if the melody had not reached its end it would not have reached its goal either. A parable."

20 ___ * _____

_____

_____

_____

20 ___ * _____

_____

_____

_____

20 ___ * _____

_____

_____

_____

20 ___ * _____

_____

_____

_____

20 ___ * _____

_____

_____

_____

29

MAY

"When your toil has been a pleasure, you have not earned money merely, but money, health, delight, and moral profit, all in one."

—*Robert Louis Stevenson*

20 ___ * _____

_____

_____

20 ___ * _____

_____

_____

20 ___ * _____

_____

_____

20 ___ * _____

_____

_____

20 ___ * _____

_____

_____

MAY

I am extremely lucky. It is my job to learn and to write, and I have tremendous freedom, every day, to decide what to do and how to do it. Yet even for me, the more room I find in my life for choosing projects that I truly love, and working toward them, the happier I become.

20 ___ * _____

_____

_____

_____

20 ___ * _____

_____

_____

_____

20 ___ * _____

_____

_____

_____

20 ___ * _____

_____

_____

_____

20 ___ * _____

_____

_____

_____

31 MAY

"The test of a vocation is the love of
the drudgery it involves."

—*Logan Pearsall Smith*

20 ___ * _____

_____

_____

_____

20 ___ * _____

_____

_____

_____

20 ___ * _____

_____

_____

_____

20 ___ * _____

_____

_____

_____

20 ___ * _____

_____

_____

_____

JUNE 1

I do best what comes naturally. When I pursue a goal that's right for me, my progress comes quickly and easily; when I pursue a goal that's wrong for me, my progress feels blocked. Now I try not to fight that sense of paralysis, but rather see it as a helpful clue to self-knowledge.

20 ___ * _____

_____

_____

_____

20 ___ * _____

_____

_____

_____

20 ___ * _____

_____

_____

_____

20 ___ * _____

_____

_____

_____

20 ___ * _____

_____

_____

_____

2 JUNE

My calendar was full of end-of-school-year
entries: "Kindergarten farewell party—bring OJ,"
"Buy teacher gift card," "Sixth-grade picnic," "Arch Day,"
and my least favorite, "Camp health forms due."
Where had the time gone?

20 ___ * _____

_____

_____

20 ___ * _____

_____

_____

20 ___ * _____

_____

_____

20 ___ * _____

_____

_____

20 ___ * _____

_____

_____

JUNE

3

"Life is a train of moods like a string of beads;
and as we pass through them they prove to be many-
colored lenses which paint the world their own hue,
and each shows only what lies in its own focus."

—*Ralph Waldo Emerson*

20 ⬭ * _____

_____

_____

20 ⬭ * _____

_____

_____

20 ⬭ * _____

_____

_____

20 ⬭ * _____

_____

_____

20 ⬭ * _____

_____

_____

4 JUNE

Although I love hearing about other people's radical happiness projects, such as Thoreau moving to Walden Pond or Elizabeth Gilbert traveling to Indonesia, I aim to find more happiness within my daily routine.

20 __ * _____

_____

_____

_____

20 __ * _____

_____

_____

_____

20 __ * _____

_____

_____

_____

20 __ * _____

_____

_____

_____

20 __ * _____

_____

_____

_____

JUNE

"A man travels the world over in search of what
he needs and returns home to find it."

—George Moore

20 ___ * _____
_____
_____
_____

20 ___ * _____
_____
_____
_____

20 ___ * _____
_____
_____
_____

20 ___ * _____
_____
_____
_____

20 ___ * _____
_____
_____
_____

JUNE

I'd heard the saying, "You're only as happy as your least happy child." The happiness of my children matters enormously to my happiness. Although I fervently want to *make* my daughters happy, I can't. They have to figure out their happiness for themselves. Nevertheless, I wanted to be as good an influence as I could be.

20 ⬭ * _____

_____

_____

_____

20 ⬭ * _____

_____

_____

_____

20 ⬭ * _____

_____

_____

_____

20 ⬭ * _____

_____

_____

_____

20 ⬭ * _____

_____

_____

_____

JUNE

"'It will be very easy to get the moon for you,' said the
Court Jester. 'I will climb the tree tonight when it gets
caught in the top branches and bring it to you.'"

—*James Thurber*, **Many Moons**

20 ⬤ * _____

_____

_____

20 ⬤ * _____

_____

_____

20 ⬤ * _____

_____

_____

20 ⬤ * _____

_____

_____

20 ⬤ * _____

_____

_____

_____

JUNE

It still took me by surprise, sometimes, to realize that these two girls were *my children*. Was I really a mother? It seemed too huge to grasp.

20 ⬭ * _____

_____

_____

20 ⬭ * _____

_____

_____

20 ⬭ * _____

_____

_____

20 ⬭ * _____

_____

_____

20 ⬭ * _____

_____

_____

JUNE

As I work on my happiness project, I keep running up
against paradoxes, and I have a paradoxical hope for my
daughters. Just as I want to accept myself and yet expect
more from myself, I want my children to dream big,
to have a grand vision for themselves, but also to accept
themselves and to take satisfaction in small things.

20 ___ * _____

_____

_____

_____

20 ___ * _____

_____

_____

_____

20 ___ * _____

_____

_____

_____

20 ___ * _____

_____

_____

_____

20 ___ * _____

_____

_____

_____

10 JUNE

My parents had never permitted unkind teasing in
the form of mockery, name-calling, or put-downs—
even when done in a joking way. At the time, I'd protested
the repression of my sarcastic remarks, which I believed
very witty, but looking back, I realize that this policy
made for a very happy atmosphere.

20 ___ * _____

_____

_____

_____

20 ___ * _____

_____

_____

_____

20 ___ * _____

_____

_____

_____

20 ___ * _____

_____

_____

_____

20 ___ * _____

_____

_____

_____

JUNE

Eye-rolling is a common, seemingly unremarkable, gesture that is highly noxious; it's one of the clearest signs of problems in a relationship. Even when eye-rolling is paired with smiles or laughter, it's a sign of contempt, intended to make a partner feel unworthy, and signals trouble.

20 ⬤ * _____

_____

_____

_____

20 ⬤ * _____

_____

_____

_____

20 ⬤ * _____

_____

_____

_____

20 ⬤ * _____

_____

_____

_____

20 ⬤ * _____

_____

_____

_____

12   JUNE

One principal reason I started my happiness project was to eliminate bad feelings from guilt, resentment, and boredom. Guilt for losing my patience with my children. Resentment toward my husband for his failure to award me gold stars. Boredom with activities that I thought I "ought" to find fun.

20 ___ * _____

_____

_____

_____

20 ___ * _____

_____

_____

_____

20 ___ * _____

_____

_____

_____

20 ___ * _____

_____

_____

_____

20 ___ * _____

_____

_____

_____

JUNE

13

"Reject your sense of injury and the
injury itself disappears."

—*Marcus Aurelius*

20 ___ * _____

_____

_____

20 ___ * _____

_____

_____

20 ___ * _____

_____

_____

20 ___ * _____

_____

_____

20 ___ * _____

_____

_____

14 JUNE

Research suggests that after the first years of marriage, a difference arises in how men and women perceive "relationship talk." Wives find relationship talk reassuring, because it makes them feel closer to their husbands; husbands find relationship talk upsetting, because they associate it with marital problems and blame.

20 ___ * _____

_____

_____

_____

20 ___ * _____

_____

_____

_____

20 ___ * _____

_____

_____

_____

20 ___ * _____

_____

_____

20 ___ * _____

_____

_____

_____

JUNE 15

Silence is sometimes more comforting than conversation. One evening, my husband seemed preoccupied, and I was ready to launch into questions like, "What's on your mind?" "Is everything okay?" "You seem distracted." Then I realized, "Actually, he really doesn't like that kind of talk," and instead, I gave him a long kiss. That seemed to cheer him up.

20 ___ * _____

_____

_____

_____

20 ___ * _____

_____

_____

_____

20 ___ * _____

_____

_____

_____

20 ___ * _____

_____

_____

_____

20 ___ * _____

_____

_____

_____

16

JUNE

Family members, colleagues, friends of both genders, and even strangers give more frequent affirmation to women than to men. Men, by contrast, depend much more on their wives for reassurance and understanding: men's relationships tend to be less intense and supportive than women's.

20 ___ * _____

_____

_____

_____

20 ___ * _____

_____

_____

_____

20 ___ * _____

_____

_____

_____

20 ___ * _____

_____

_____

_____

20 ___ * _____

_____

_____

_____

JUNE 17

I try to say the words "I love you" more often.
People are more apt to feel close to a family member who
often expresses affection than one who rarely does.

20 ___ * _____

_____

_____

20 ___ * _____

_____

_____

20 ___ * _____

_____

_____

20 ___ * _____

_____

_____

20 ___ * _____

_____

_____

18 JUNE

Experts advise parents to establish routines and rituals to provide children with a feeling of predictability, order, and connection. But adults crave these things, too. I resolved to make a ritual to "Kiss in the morning, kiss at night."

20 ___ * _____

_____

_____

_____

20 ___ * _____

_____

_____

_____

20 ___ * _____

_____

_____

_____

20 ___ * _____

_____

_____

_____

20 ___ * _____

_____

_____

_____

JUNE

19

"Habit simplifies our movements, makes them
accurate, and diminishes fatigue."

—William James

20 ___ * _____

_____

_____

_____

20 ___ * _____

_____

_____

_____

20 ___ * _____

_____

_____

_____

20 ___ * _____

_____

_____

_____

20 ___ * _____

_____

_____

_____

20   JUNE

I've always been drawn to libraries; I love the sense of possibility and industry, the quiet company, and *all those books*. In college, whenever I was feeling blue, I'd pick a floor in the library at random and explore among the crowded, mysterious shelves. That always gave me a feeling of excitement and adventure.

20 ___ * _____

_____

_____

_____

20 ___ * _____

_____

_____

_____

20 ___ * _____

_____

_____

_____

20 ___ * _____

_____

_____

_____

20 ___ * _____

_____

_____

_____

JUNE

One key lesson I've learned from my happiness project
is to pay close attention to any flame of enthusiasm.
In the past, I'd often ignored a surge of interest. I've come
to realize, however, that I don't have so many passions
or enthusiasms that I can afford to ignore any of them.

20 ___ * _____

_____

_____

20 ___ * _____

_____

_____

20 ___ * _____

_____

_____

20 ___ * _____

_____

_____

20 ___ * _____

_____

_____

22 JUNE

I used to tell myself, "I should learn more about art. It's beautiful, it's interesting, it's fun!" But I somehow couldn't figure out how to approach it. When I paid close attention to what I looked at with pleasure—not what I thought I *should* like, but what I actually *did* like— I found my obsession and the way to pursue it.

20 ⬭ * _____

_____

_____

_____

20 ⬭ * _____

_____

_____

_____

20 ⬭ * _____

_____

_____

_____

20 ⬭ * _____

_____

_____

_____

20 ⬭ * _____

_____

_____

_____

JUNE

"The way is not in the sky. The way is in the heart."

—*Buddha*

20 __ * _____

_____

_____

20 __ * _____

_____

_____

20 __ * _____

_____

_____

20 __ * _____

_____

_____

20 __ * _____

_____

_____

24 JUNE

After I'd realized that I loved miniatures, I saw that I'd loved them my whole life. When I identified the pattern in many things that caught my eye—*miniatures*—I was able to embrace and build on a passion that I'd somehow never even noticed before, a love of doll houses, birdhouses, bonsai, model villages, aquariums and terrariums.

20 ___ * _____

_____

_____

_____

20 ___ * _____

_____

_____

_____

20 ___ * _____

_____

_____

_____

20 ___ * _____

_____

_____

_____

20 ___ * _____

_____

_____

_____

JUNE

25

"The Little House was very happy as she sat on the hill and watched the countryside around her. She watched the sun rise in the morning and she watched the sun set in the evening. Day followed day, each one a little different from the one before . . . but the Little House stayed just the same."

—*Virginia Lee Burton,* **The Little House**

20 ⬤ __ * _____

_____

_____

_____

20 ⬤ __ * _____

_____

_____

_____

20 ⬤ __ * _____

_____

_____

_____

20 ⬤ __ * _____

_____

_____

_____

20 ⬤ __ * _____

_____

_____

_____

26 JUNE

People getting along harmoniously—in a family, among friends, or in an office—make an effort to enter into the interests of one another's lives.

20 ___ * _____
_____
_____
_____

20 ___ * _____
_____
_____
_____

20 ___ * _____
_____
_____
_____

20 ___ * _____
_____
_____
_____

20 ___ * _____
_____
_____

JUNE

27

"The true spirit of conversation consists more in bringing out the cleverness of others than in showing a great deal of it yourself; he who goes away pleased with himself and his own wit is also greatly pleased with you."

—*Jean de La Bruyère*

20 ⬭ * _____

_____

_____

_____

20 ⬭ * _____

_____

_____

_____

20 ⬭ * _____

_____

_____

_____

20 ⬭ * _____

_____

_____

_____

20 ⬭ * _____

_____

_____

_____

28

JUNE

Children crave to be taken seriously. I remember one
afternoon when my mother was driving me to the library,
and I was enthusiastically describing some book. My
mother said, "Don't return it yet. If it's that good, I want
to read it." I was thrilled. My mother was going to
read a book because *I'd* recommended it!

20 ___ * _____

_____

_____

_____

20 ___ * _____

_____

_____

_____

20 ___ * _____

_____

_____

_____

20 ___ * _____

_____

_____

_____

20 ___ * _____

_____

_____

_____

JUNE 29

"He told his mother all about his adventures while she took off his wet socks. And he thought and thought and thought about them."

— *Ezra Jack Keats*, **The Snowy Day**

20 ___ * _____

_____

_____

_____

20 ___ * _____

_____

_____

_____

20 ___ * _____

_____

_____

_____

20 ___ * _____

_____

_____

_____

20 ___ * _____

_____

_____

_____

30 JUNE

I frequently engage in two complementary tasks: first, to identify, arrange, and spotlight meaningful possessions; second, to get rid of meaningless stuff.

20 ___ * _____

_____

_____

20 ___ * _____

_____

_____

20 ___ * _____

_____

_____

20 ___ * _____

_____

_____

20 ___ * _____

_____

_____

JULY 1

If something's important to you, you should reserve time for it in your schedule, make a place for it in your home, and build relationships around it.

20 ___ * _____

_____

_____

20 ___ * _____

_____

_____

20 ___ * _____

_____

_____

20 ___ * _____

_____

_____

20 ___ * _____

_____

_____

2

JULY

A common source of conflict among siblings is competition for their parents' attention. Although my daughters get along very well, both girls appreciate the chance to be alone in the spotlight. I also want to have regular opportunities to be alone with each girl, doing the activities she loves without any interruptions.

20 ___ * _____

_____

_____

20 ___ * _____

_____

_____

20 ___ * _____

_____

_____

20 ___ * _____

_____

_____

20 ___ * _____

_____

_____

JULY 3

The days are long, but the years are short. Already, sunglasses, *The Hunger Games,* iTunes, and dried seaweed had replaced headbands, *The Wizard of Oz,* Laurie Berkner, and Pez. *Now* was the time to spend Wednesday afternoons with my daughter.

20 ___ * _____

_____

_____

20 ___ * _____

_____

_____

20 ___ * _____

_____

_____

20 ___ * _____

_____

_____

20 ___ * _____

_____

_____

JULY 4

According to research, interrupting a pleasant experience with something less pleasant can intensify a person's overall pleasure; for example, surprisingly, commercials make TV-watching more fun, and interrupting a massage heightens the pleasure it gives.

20 __ __ * _____

_____

_____

_____

20 __ __ * _____

_____

_____

_____

20 __ __ * _____

_____

_____

_____

20 __ __ * _____

_____

_____

_____

20 __ __ * _____

_____

_____

_____

JULY

Along with my vacation pleasure reading, I brought
several long articles, and every day, I read one. As the studies predicted, this small, daily irksome task made vacation
more fun. It amplified my general feeling of leisure; when
I was reading for fun, it felt more fun. Also, tackling this
work made me feel virtuous and productive.

20 ___ * _____

_____

_____

_____

20 ___ * _____

_____

_____

_____

20 ___ * _____

_____

_____

_____

20 ___ * _____

_____

_____

_____

20 ___ * _____

_____

_____

_____

6   JULY

Here are the Secrets of Adulthood that came in handy during a family vacation: Start early if possible. Don't let anyone get too hungry. Remind kids to visit the bathroom. Quit while you're ahead. The point is to *have fun*.

20 ___ * _____

_____

_____

_____

20 ___ * _____

_____

_____

_____

20 ___ * _____

_____

_____

_____

20 ___ * _____

_____

_____

_____

20 ___ * _____

_____

_____

_____

JULY

"Plans are worthless, but planning is everything."

—*Dwight D. Eisenhower*

20 ___ * _____

_____

_____

_____

20 ___ * _____

_____

_____

_____

20 ___ * _____

_____

_____

_____

20 ___ * _____

_____

_____

_____

20 ___ * _____

_____

_____

_____

JULY

An important exercise for happiness is to look
for ways to eliminate the causes of unhappiness,
or if that isn't possible, to deal constructively
with negative emotions and difficult situations.

20 ⬭ * _____

_____

_____

_____

20 ⬭ * _____

_____

_____

_____

20 ⬭ * _____

_____

_____

_____

20 ⬭ * _____

_____

_____

_____

20 ⬭ * _____

_____

_____

_____

JULY

"Holding on to anger is like grasping a hot coal
with the intent of throwing it at someone else;
you are the one who gets burned."

—Buddha

20 ___ * _____

_____

_____

20 ___ * _____

_____

_____

20 ___ * _____

_____

_____

20 ___ * _____

_____

_____

20 ___ * _____

_____

_____

10

JULY

As the counterpart to giving my husband more gold stars,
I also try to stop giving him black marks; I've discovered,
however, that I have an easier time saying nice things than
biting back critical comments. I enjoy saying, "Thanks" or
"What a great solution," but find it hard to resist saying,
"Haven't you done that yet?" or "You're not being helpful."

20 ___ * _____

_____

_____

_____

20 ___ * _____

_____

_____

_____

20 ___ * _____

_____

_____

_____

20 ___ * _____

_____

_____

_____

20 ___ * _____

_____

_____

_____

JULY

"I would like to become tolerant without overlooking anything, persecute no one even when all people persecute me;
become better without noticing it; become sadder, but enjoy
living; become more serene, be happy in others; belong to
no one, grow in everyone; love the best, comfort the worst;
not even hate myself anymore." —*Elias Canetti*

20 __ * _____

_____

_____

_____

20 __ * _____

_____

_____

_____

20 __ * _____

_____

_____

_____

20 __ * _____

_____

_____

_____

20 __ * _____

_____

_____

_____

12 JULY

In "unconscious overclaiming," we unconsciously overestimate our contributions or skills relative to other people. According to research, when wives and husbands estimated what percentage of housework each performed on her or his own, the percentages added up to more than 120 percent.

20 ___ * _____

_____

_____

_____

20 ___ * _____

_____

_____

_____

20 ___ * _____

_____

_____

_____

20 ___ * _____

_____

_____

_____

20 ___ * _____

_____

_____

_____

JULY 13

If you make positive statements, you may help persuade yourself and other people to take a positive view of things. If you make negative statements, you do the opposite. For example, if I say, "Wow, we got so much done around the apartment today," my husband and I are both prompted to think that we got a lot done.

20 __ * _____

_____

_____

_____

20 __ * _____

_____

_____

_____

20 __ * _____

_____

_____

_____

20 __ * _____

_____

_____

_____

20 __ * _____

_____

_____

_____

14 JULY

"Enough is abundance to the wise."

—Euripides

20 ⬭ __ * _____

_____

_____

_____

20 ⬭ __ * _____

_____

_____

_____

20 ⬭ __ * _____

_____

_____

_____

20 ⬭ __ * _____

_____

_____

_____

20 ⬭ __ * _____

_____

_____

_____

JULY

15

To make your home a place of comfort and vitality, strive
not merely to eliminate. "Plainness was not necessarily
simplicity," Frank Lloyd Wright cautioned. "To know what
to leave out and what to put in; just where and just how, ah,
that is to have been educated in knowledge of simplicity."

20 ___ * _____

_____

_____

_____

20 ___ * _____

_____

_____

_____

20 ___ * _____

_____

_____

_____

20 ___ * _____

_____

_____

_____

20 ___ * _____

_____

_____

_____

16 JULY

I've often felt a yearning to escape from the ties of ownership. I've wanted to dump the entire contents of a chest of drawers into the trash rather than endure the headache of sorting the good from the bad. I often choose not to buy something useful or beautiful, because I don't want the responsibility of another possession.

20 ___ * _____

_____

_____

_____

20 ___ * _____

_____

_____

_____

20 ___ * _____

_____

_____

_____

20 ___ * _____

_____

_____

_____

20 ___ * _____

_____

_____

_____

JULY

Sometimes, in an eerie, dark reversal, I love
something so much that I feel the urge to destroy it,
to be free from that attachment and the fear of loss.

20 ___ * _____

_____

_____

20 ___ * _____

_____

_____

20 ___ * _____

_____

_____

20 ___ * _____

_____

_____

20 ___ * _____

_____

_____

18 JULY

I feel a powerful connection to things I associate with my daughters. Occasionally, getting rid of a childhood relic like a diaper pail was a joy, but more often, I felt a sense of loss. Also, the longer I held on to things, the more sentiment attached to them.

20 ___ * _____

_____

_____

_____

20 ___ * _____

_____

_____

_____

20 ___ * _____

_____

_____

_____

20 ___ * _____

_____

_____

_____

20 ___ * _____

_____

_____

_____

JULY

19

While sorting through the things that my daughters had outgrown, I noticed that when I consciously permitted myself to save a particular thing, I was able to get rid of more stuff; carefully preserving a few pieces of artwork meant that I didn't have to keep every drawing.

20 ___ * _____

_____

_____

_____

20 ___ * _____

_____

_____

_____

20 ___ * _____

_____

_____

_____

20 ___ * _____

_____

_____

_____

20 ___ * _____

_____

_____

_____

20

JULY

"Happiness is a place between
too much and too little."

—*Finnish proverb*

20 ___ * _____

_____

_____

_____

20 ___ * _____

_____

_____

_____

20 ___ * _____

_____

_____

_____

20 ___ * _____

_____

_____

_____

20 ___ * _____

_____

_____

_____

JULY

21

Someplace, keep an empty shelf;
someplace, keep a junk drawer.

20 ___ * _____

_____

_____

_____

20 ___ * _____

_____

_____

_____

20 ___ * _____

_____

_____

_____

20 ___ * _____

_____

_____

_____

20 ___ * _____

_____

_____

_____

22 JULY

Underreacting to little household accidents
makes them less irritating, because after all, they're
only as annoying as we allow them to be.

20 ___ * _____

_____

_____

_____

20 ___ * _____

_____

_____

_____

20 ___ * _____

_____

_____

_____

20 ___ * _____

_____

_____

_____

20 ___ * _____

_____

_____

_____

JULY

23

One of the most effective ways to help myself underreact is to joke around. Over and over I find that if I act light-hearted, I'll feel more light-hearted. But when I feel irritated, my sense of humor deserts me.

20 ___ * _____

_____

_____

_____

20 ___ * _____

_____

_____

_____

20 ___ * _____

_____

_____

_____

20 ___ * _____

_____

_____

_____

20 ___ * _____

_____

_____

_____

24

JULY

Never forget how easy it is to forget.

20 ___ * _____

_____

_____

20 ___ * _____

_____

_____

_____

20 ___ * _____

_____

_____

_____

20 ___ * _____

_____

_____

_____

20 ___ * _____

_____

_____

_____

JULY

25

"The one serious conviction that a man should have
is that nothing is to be taken too seriously."

—*Samuel Butler*

20 ___ * _____

_____

_____

_____

20 ___ * _____

_____

_____

_____

20 ___ * _____

_____

_____

_____

20 ___ * _____

_____

_____

_____

20 ___ * _____

_____

_____

_____

26   JULY

Lightheartedness is a very helpful quality. Showing levity is less about being funny and more about being able to have fun and see the humorous side of everyday situations—especially difficult situations.

20 ___ * _____

_____

_____

_____

20 ___ * _____

_____

_____

_____

20 ___ * _____

_____

_____

_____

20 ___ * _____

_____

_____

_____

20 ___ * _____

_____

_____

_____

JULY

27

"It is easy to be heavy; hard to be light."

— *G.K. Chesterton*

20 ___ *_____

_____

_____

_____

20 ___ *_____

_____

_____

_____

20 ___ *_____

_____

_____

_____

20 ___ *_____

_____

_____

_____

20 ___ *_____

_____

_____

_____

28 JULY

Why, I often wonder, is it difficult to push myself to do the things that bring happiness? Every day, I struggle to give a kiss, to get enough sleep, to stop checking my e-mail, to give gold stars. Every day, I remind myself to accept myself, and expect more from myself.

20 ___ * _____

20 ___ * _____

20 ___ * _____

20 ___ * _____

20 ___ * _____

JULY

29

"Who is strong? He that can conquer his bad habits."

—*Benjamin Franklin*

20 ___ * _____

_____

_____

_____

20 ___ * _____

_____

_____

_____

20 ___ * _____

_____

_____

_____

20 ___ * _____

_____

_____

_____

20 ___ * _____

_____

_____

_____

30 JULY

Some of the great minds in history urge us toward simplicity. Thoreau admonished, "Our life is frittered away by detail. . . . Simplicity, simplicity, simplicity!"

20 ___ * _____

_____

_____

_____

20 ___ * _____

_____

_____

_____

20 ___ * _____

_____

_____

_____

20 ___ * _____

_____

_____

_____

20 ___ * _____

_____

_____

_____

JULY

"Life is barren enough surely with all her trappings," warned Samuel Johnson, "let us therefore be cautious how we strip her."

20 ___ * _____

_____

_____

20 ___ * _____

_____

_____

20 ___ * _____

_____

_____

20 ___ * _____

_____

_____

20 ___ * _____

_____

_____

1 | AUGUST

My home is a reflection of myself, so the work I do to make my home more homey is actually an extended exercise in self-knowledge. To be more at home at home, I have to know myself, and face myself. *This* is the way to true simplicity: to be myself, free from affectation, posturing, or defensiveness.

20 ⬭ * _____

_____

_____

_____

20 ⬭ * _____

_____

_____

_____

20 ⬭ * _____

_____

_____

_____

20 ⬭ * _____

_____

_____

_____

20 ⬭ * _____

_____

_____

_____

AUGUST

2

"It is hard, so terribly hard, to please yourself. Far from being the easy thing that it sounds like, it is almost the hardest thing in the world, because we are not always comfortable with that true self that lies deep within us."

—Christopher Alexander

20 __ * _____

_____

_____

20 __ * _____

_____

_____

20 __ * _____

_____

_____

20 __ * _____

_____

_____

20 __ * _____

_____

_____

AUGUST

In my home, I wanted the peace of simplicity, of space
and order; but I had to guard against my impulse
to toss out every item in the refrigerator. I wanted the
sense of ampleness and possibility, with beloved objects,
plentiful supplies, and a luxuriant disarray.

20 ___ * _____

_____

_____

_____

20 ___ * _____

_____

_____

_____

20 ___ * _____

_____

_____

_____

20 ___ * _____

_____

_____

_____

20 ___ * _____

_____

_____

_____

AUGUST

"Everything should be made as simple
as possible, but not simpler."

—*Albert Einstein*

20 ___ * _____

_____

_____

_____

20 ___ * _____

_____

_____

_____

20 ___ * _____

_____

_____

_____

20 ___ * _____

_____

_____

_____

20 ___ * _____

_____

_____

_____

5 AUGUST

Declaring that we'd all be happy with more, or with less, is like saying that every book should be a hundred pages long. Every book has a right length, and people differ in the number of possessions, and the types of possessions, with which they can meaningfully engage. There's no one right way; you must decide what's right for *you*.

20 ___ * _____

_____

_____

_____

20 ___ * _____

_____

_____

_____

20 ___ * _____

_____

_____

_____

20 ___ * _____

_____

_____

_____

20 ___ * _____

_____

_____

_____

AUGUST

"Nobody in my family is fancy at all. They never even ask for sprinkles. There's a lot they don't understand. . . . Lace-trimmed socks *do* help me to play soccer better. Sandwiches *definitely* taste better when you stick in frilly toothpicks."

—*Jane O'Connor,* **Fancy Nancy**

20 ___ * _____

_____

_____

_____

20 ___ * _____

_____

_____

_____

20 ___ * _____

_____

_____

_____

20 ___ * _____

_____

_____

_____

20 ___ * _____

_____

_____

_____

7

AUGUST

Cultivating your possessions, then, isn't a simple
matter of organization, elimination, or accumulation;
it is a matter of engagement. When you feel engaged with
your possessions, you feel enlivened by them, and when
you feel disengaged from them, you feel burdened.

20 ___ * _____

_____

_____

_____

20 ___ * _____

_____

_____

_____

20 ___ * _____

_____

_____

_____

20 ___ * _____

_____

_____

_____

20 ___ * _____

_____

_____

_____

AUGUST

With my resolution to "Cultivate a shrine," I meant
to transform areas of my apartment into places of
super-engagement. By "shrine," I didn't mean a niche
with candles, flowers, and a statue, but rather, an area
that enshrined my passions, interests, and values.
A shrine is a sign of dedication.

20 ___ * _____

_____

_____

_____

20 ___ * _____

_____

_____

_____

20 ___ * _____

_____

_____

_____

20 ___ * _____

_____

_____

_____

20 ___ * _____

_____

_____

_____

9 AUGUST

I decided to create a Shrine to Fun and Games by filling a bookcase with board games, puzzles, five glass apothecary jars filled with tiny toys that didn't belong anyplace, toys that I'd saved from my own childhood, and the lovely silver rattles that my daughters had received as baby gifts.

20 ___ * _____

_____

_____

_____

20 ___ * _____

_____

_____

_____

20 ___ * _____

_____

_____

_____

20 ___ * _____

_____

_____

_____

20 ___ * _____

_____

_____

_____

AUGUST 10

"The creative mind plays with the objects it loves."

—*Carl Jung*

20 ___ * _____

_____

_____

_____

20 ___ * _____

_____

_____

_____

20 ___ * _____

_____

_____

_____

20 ___ * _____

_____

_____

_____

20 ___ * _____

_____

_____

_____

11 | AUGUST

I love my office because I love working, but the room itself wasn't particularly pleasing. I'd never tried to make it beautiful and distinctive. I decided to make my office more shrinelike; after all, I probably spent more of my waking hours in my office than in any other room in the apartment.

20 ___ * _____

_____

_____

_____

20 ___ * _____

_____

_____

_____

20 ___ * _____

_____

_____

_____

20 ___ * _____

_____

_____

_____

20 ___ * _____

_____

_____

_____

AUGUST 12

Once I started cultivating my shrines, I began to notice that other people, consciously or unconsciously, had constructed their own. Some familiar shrines are the Shrines to Music, Shrines to Travel, or Shrines to Tools. For many people, a car is an important shrine; a bathroom can also be a shrine.

20 ___ * _____

_____

_____

_____

20 ___ * _____

_____

_____

_____

20 ___ * _____

_____

_____

_____

20 ___ * _____

_____

_____

_____

20 ___ * _____

_____

_____

_____

13 AUGUST

The power of objects doesn't depend on their volume; in fact, my memories are better evoked by a few carefully chosen items than by a big assortment of things with vague associations. Whenever I look at the two bird figurines inherited from my beloved grandparents, our long relationship is embodied in a few small objects.

20 ___ * _____

_____

_____

_____

20 ___ * _____

_____

_____

_____

20 ___ * _____

_____

_____

_____

20 ___ * _____

_____

_____

_____

20 ___ * _____

_____

_____

_____

AUGUST

14

"When they had eventually calmed down a bit,
and had gotten home, Mr. Duncan put the magic pebble
in an iron safe. Some day they might want to use it,
but really, for now, what more could they wish for?
They all had all that they wanted."

—*William Steig,* **Sylvester and the Magic Pebble**

20 ___ * _____

_____

_____

20 ___ * _____

_____

_____

20 ___ * _____

_____

_____

20 ___ * _____

_____

_____

20 ___ * _____

_____

_____

15 AUGUST

Outer order contributes to inner calm. Why? Perhaps because it gives you a tangible sense of control, or relief from visual noise, or release from guilt.

20 ___ * _____

20 ___ * _____

20 ___ * _____

20 ___ * _____

20 ___ * _____

AUGUST

16

Mise en place is a French cooking term for "everything in its place." Mise en place describes the preparation done before starting the actual cooking, such as chopping, measuring, gathering ingredients and implements. Mise en place is preparation, but it's also a state of mind. Nothing is more satisfying than working easily and well.

20 ___ * _____

_____

_____

20 ___ * _____

_____

_____

20 ___ * _____

_____

_____

20 ___ * _____

_____

_____

20 ___ * _____

_____

_____

17

AUGUST

"Order is Heaven's first law."

—*Alexander Pope*

20 ___ * _____

_____

_____

_____

20 ___ * _____

_____

_____

_____

20 ___ * _____

_____

_____

_____

20 ___ * _____

_____

_____

_____

20 ___ * _____

_____

_____

_____

AUGUST

18

Everything looks better arranged on a tray.

20 ⬤ * _____

_____

_____

_____

20 ⬤ * _____

_____

_____

_____

20 ⬤ * _____

_____

_____

_____

20 ⬤ * _____

_____

_____

_____

20 ⬤ * _____

_____

_____

_____

19

AUGUST

SECRETS OF ADULTHOOD: Discard a pen or magic marker as soon as it runs dry. Replace a lightbulb or an empty roll of toilet paper right away. Keep pens, a notepad, and a pair of scissors in every room. Always keep your keys in the same place.

20 ___ * _____

_____

_____

_____

20 ___ * _____

_____

_____

_____

20 ___ * _____

_____

_____

_____

20 ___ * _____

_____

_____

_____

20 ___ * _____

_____

_____

_____

AUGUST

"One can have no smaller or greater
mastery than mastery of oneself."

— *Leonardo da Vinci*

20 ___ * _____

_____

_____

_____

20 ___ * _____

_____

_____

_____

20 ___ * _____

_____

_____

_____

20 ___ * _____

_____

_____

_____

20 ___ * _____

_____

_____

_____

21 AUGUST

For the most part, I don't focus on the happiness differences between men and women, because I think it obscures the differences among individuals. When I focus on the way "men" or "husbands" generally behave, I start to lump my husband along with half of humanity. I find myself feeling angry or annoyed with him for things he hasn't even done.

20 ___ * _____

_____

_____

_____

20 ___ * _____

_____

_____

_____

20 ___ * _____

_____

_____

_____

20 ___ * _____

_____

_____

_____

20 ___ * _____

_____

_____

_____

AUGUST

I thank my husband when he tackles some chore, even if it was something he was "supposed" to do. When he solves a problem for me, or gives me useful advice, I tell him how helpful he's been, instead of taking him for granted.

20 ⬚ * _____

_____

_____

_____

20 ⬚ * _____

_____

_____

_____

20 ⬚ * _____

_____

_____

_____

20 ⬚ * _____

_____

_____

_____

20 ⬚ * _____

_____

_____

_____

23 AUGUST

When my husband calls me, I try to sound
pleased and engaged, not rushed or distracted.
I don't attempt to read e-mails while talking to him
on the phone. (So rude! But I've done it. Often.)

20 ___ * _____

_____

_____

_____

20 ___ * _____

_____

_____

_____

20 ___ * _____

_____

_____

_____

20 ___ * _____

_____

_____

_____

20 ___ * _____

_____

_____

_____

AUGUST

"Men's natures are alike; it is their
habits that separate them."

—*Confucius*

20 ___ *_____

_____

_____

_____

20 ___ *_____

_____

_____

_____

20 ___ *_____

_____

_____

_____

20 ___ *_____

_____

_____

_____

20 ___ *_____

_____

_____

_____

25 AUGUST

"Exuberance is beauty."

—*William Blake*

20 ___ * _____

_____

_____

_____

20 ___ * _____

_____

_____

_____

20 ___ * _____

_____

_____

_____

20 ___ * _____

_____

_____

_____

20 ___ * _____

_____

_____

_____

AUGUST 26

Studies show that happy couples are much more likely to idealize each other, and by holding those positive perceptions, they help each other live up to them. When romantic partners expect the best in each other, they help each other attain those ideals.

20 ___ * _____

_____

_____

_____

20 ___ * _____

_____

_____

_____

20 ___ * _____

_____

_____

_____

20 ___ * _____

_____

_____

_____

20 ___ * _____

_____

_____

_____

27 AUGUST

"If you make it a habit not to blame others, you will feel the growth of the ability to love in your soul, and you will see the growth of goodness in your life."

— *Leo Tolstoy*

20 ___ * _____

_____

_____

_____

20 ___ * _____

_____

_____

_____

20 ___ * _____

_____

_____

_____

20 ___ * _____

_____

_____

_____

20 ___ * _____

_____

_____

_____

AUGUST

28

If my husband asks, "Will you do me a favor?"
I attempt to bite back an automatic negative response,
or a suspicious, "What's the favor?"

20 __ * _____

_____

_____

20 __ * _____

_____

_____

20 __ * _____

_____

_____

20 __ * _____

_____

_____

20 __ * _____

_____

_____

29 AUGUST

One late-summer Sunday evening, I felt overwhelmed by a familiar but surprising emotion: I was homesick, I realized, with a prospective nostalgia for now and here—when my husband and I live with our two girls under our roof, with our own parents strong and busy, everyone healthy, and no disaster looming except the woes of sixth grade.

20 ___ * _____

_____

_____

_____

20 ___ * _____

_____

_____

_____

20 ___ * _____

_____

_____

_____

20 ___ * _____

_____

_____

_____

20 ___ * _____

_____

_____

_____

AUGUST 30

"Happiness, knowledge, not in another place, but this place,
not for another hour but this hour . . ."

—*Walt Whitman*

20 ___ * _____

_____

_____

_____

20 ___ * _____

_____

_____

_____

20 ___ * _____

_____

_____

_____

20 ___ * _____

_____

_____

_____

20 ___ * _____

_____

_____

_____

31 AUGUST

"They always say that time changes things,
but you actually have to change them yourself."

—*Andy Warhol*

20 __ * _____

_____

_____

_____

20 __ * _____

_____

_____

_____

20 __ * _____

_____

_____

_____

20 __ * _____

_____

_____

_____

20 __ * _____

_____

_____

_____

SEPTEMBER

September marks the start of a new year, with the empty calendar and clean slate of the next school cycle. Even if you are no longer in school yourself, September neverthe-less remains charged with possibility and renewal. It is also the season of the Mother Olympics; it is hard to keep track of everything that you have to buy, fill out, or turn in.

20 ___ * _____

_____

_____

_____

20 ___ * _____

_____

_____

_____

20 ___ * _____

_____

_____

_____

20 ___ * _____

_____

_____

_____

20 ___ * _____

_____

_____

_____

2 SEPTEMBER

Although research shows that novelty and challenge boost happiness, when I started my study of happiness, I was convinced that this wasn't true for me. For me, I believed, familiarity and mastery were keys to happiness. But when I pushed myself, I discovered—no! Even for someone like me, novelty and challenge serve as huge engines of happiness.

20 ___ * _____

_____

_____

_____

20 ___ * _____

_____

_____

_____

20 ___ * _____

_____

_____

_____

20 ___ * _____

_____

_____

_____

20 ___ * _____

_____

_____

_____

SEPTEMBER

"To be what we are, and to become what we are capable
of becoming, is the only end of life."

—*Robert Louis Stevenson*

20 ___ * _____

_____

_____

20 ___ * _____

_____

_____

20 ___ * _____

_____

_____

20 ___ * _____

_____

_____

20 ___ * _____

_____

_____

4 SEPTEMBER

When an experience is new or challenging, and
we must absorb more information, time seems to pass
more slowly; when one day blurs indistinguishably
from the last, the months evaporate.

20 ___ * _____

_____

_____

_____

20 ___ * _____

_____

_____

_____

20 ___ * _____

_____

_____

_____

20 ___ * _____

_____

_____

_____

20 ___ * _____

_____

_____

_____

SEPTEMBER 5

Persistence is more important to mastery than
innate ability, because the single most important element in
developing an expertise is the willingness to practice.

20 ___ * _____

_____

_____

20 ___ * _____

_____

_____

20 ___ * _____

_____

_____

20 ___ * _____

_____

_____

20 ___ * _____

_____

_____

SEPTEMBER

While you can make a child practice,
you can't make a child *want* to practice.

20 ___ * _____

_____

_____

_____

20 ___ * _____

_____

_____

_____

20 ___ * _____

_____

_____

_____

20 ___ * _____

_____

_____

_____

20 ___ * _____

_____

_____

_____

SEPTEMBER

"The least strained and most natural ways
of the soul are the most beautiful; the best
occupations are the least forced."

—Montaigne

20 ___ * _____

_____

_____

_____

20 ___ * _____

_____

_____

_____

20 ___ * _____

_____

_____

_____

20 ___ * _____

_____

_____

_____

20 ___ * _____

_____

_____

_____

8 SEPTEMBER

Although we often enjoy activities more when we're good at them, facility doesn't guarantee enjoyment, whether in work or play. In fact, being good at something can sometimes mask the fact that it's not enjoyable.

20 ___ * _____

_____

_____

_____

20 ___ * _____

_____

_____

_____

20 ___ * _____

_____

_____

_____

20 ___ * _____

_____

_____

_____

20 ___ * _____

_____

_____

_____

SEPTEMBER

Self-discipline for the sake of self-discipline seems an arid pursuit. As Samuel Johnson observed, "All severity that does not tend to increase good, or prevent evil, is idle."

20 __ * _____

_____

_____

20 __ * _____

_____

_____

20 __ * _____

_____

_____

20 __ * _____

_____

_____

20 __ * _____

_____

_____

10 SEPTEMBER

Now that I'm a parent, I marvel at the encouragement
my own parents gave me when I decided to leave law to
try to become a writer; it's painful to see your children risk
failure or disappointment, or pursue activities that seem
like a waste of time, effort, and money. But we parents
don't really know what's safe or a waste of time.

20 ___ * _____

_____

_____

_____

20 ___ * _____

_____

_____

_____

20 ___ * _____

_____

_____

_____

20 ___ * _____

_____

_____

_____

20 ___ * _____

_____

_____

_____

SEPTEMBER

11

"His mother saw that he was not lonesome, and because she was an understanding mother, even though she was a cow, she let him just sit there and be happy."

—*Munro Leaf,* **The Story of Ferdinand**

20 ⬭ * _____

_____

_____

_____

20 ⬭ * _____

_____

_____

_____

20 ⬭ * _____

_____

_____

_____

20 ⬭ * _____

_____

_____

_____

20 ⬭ * _____

_____

_____

_____

12 SEPTEMBER

The credential-hoarding, college-admissions–
minded part of me wants to see my daughter accumulate
accomplishments, but the wiser part of me argues that
one of the most important lessons of childhood is
discovering what you *like* to do.

20 ___ * _____

_____

_____

_____

20 ___ * _____

_____

_____

_____

20 ___ * _____

_____

_____

_____

20 ___ * _____

_____

_____

_____

20 ___ * _____

_____

_____

_____

SEPTEMBER 13

"I think periods of browsing during which no occupation is imposed from without are important in youth because they give time for the formation of these apparently fugitive but really vital impressions."

—*Bertrand Russell*

20 ___ * _____

_____

_____

20 ___ * _____

_____

_____

20 ___ * _____

_____

_____

20 ___ * _____

_____

_____

20 ___ * _____

_____

_____

14 SEPTEMBER

"She thought to herself, 'If only I had a child as white as snow, as red as blood, and her hair as dark as ebony.'"

—*Brothers Grimm*, **Snow White**

20 ⬤ __ * _____

_____

_____

_____

20 ⬤ __ * _____

_____

_____

_____

20 ⬤ __ * _____

_____

_____

_____

20 ⬤ __ * _____

_____

_____

_____

20 ⬤ __ * _____

_____

_____

SEPTEMBER 15

"See the child you have," as the saying goes,
"not the child you wish you had."

20 ___ * _____

_____

_____

_____

20 ___ * _____

_____

_____

_____

20 ___ * _____

_____

_____

_____

20 ___ * _____

_____

_____

_____

20 ___ * _____

_____

_____

_____

16 SEPTEMBER

A happiness paradox: control and mastery bring happiness; so do surprises, novelty, and challenge. In fact, positive events make us happier when they're not predictable, because the surprise makes the experience more intense.

20 ___ * _____

_____

_____

_____

20 ___ * _____

_____

_____

_____

20 ___ * _____

_____

_____

_____

20 ___ * _____

_____

_____

_____

20 ___ * _____

_____

_____

_____

SEPTEMBER 17

Studies show that we react more strongly to an unexpected pleasure than to an expected one. The brain gets a bigger thrill when some little treat comes as a surprise, whether it's a dollar found in the street, a free cookie, or a compliment from a boss. These little boosts of happiness make us temporarily smarter, friendlier, and more productive.

20 ___ * _____

_____

_____

_____

20 ___ * _____

_____

_____

_____

20 ___ * _____

_____

_____

_____

20 ___ * _____

_____

_____

_____

20 ___ * _____

_____

_____

_____

18 SEPTEMBER

What nice little surprises could I plan for my
parents and in-laws? I knew they loved any updates
about the girls, so I made a bigger effort to report after
a teacher's conference or doctor's appointment and to
pass along particularly funny or sweet remarks.

20 ___ * _____

_____

_____

_____

20 ___ * _____

_____

_____

_____

20 ___ * _____

_____

_____

_____

20 ___ * _____

_____

_____

_____

20 ___ * _____

_____

_____

_____

SEPTEMBER 19

"With what pleasure do we look upon a family, through the whole of which reign mutual love and esteem, where the parents and children are companions for one another, without any other difference than what is made by respectful affection on the one side, and kind indulgence on the other . . ."

—Adam Smith

20 ⬭ * _____

_____

_____

_____

20 ⬭ * _____

_____

_____

_____

20 ⬭ * _____

_____

_____

_____

20 ⬭ * _____

_____

_____

_____

20 ⬭ * _____

_____

_____

_____

20 SEPTEMBER

Studies show that doing something "exciting" (something a couple doesn't usually do, like biking, for example) gives a bigger romantic boost than doing something "pleasant" (such as going to a movie). Novelty and excitement stimulate the brain chemicals that are present during courtship.

20 ___ * _____

_____

_____

_____

20 ___ * _____

_____

_____

_____

20 ___ * _____

_____

_____

_____

20 ___ * _____

_____

_____

_____

20 ___ * _____

_____

_____

_____

SEPTEMBER

21

Anticipation, as well as surprise, is an
important element of happiness.

20 ⬭ * _____

_____

_____

_____

20 ⬭ * _____

_____

_____

_____

20 ⬭ * _____

_____

_____

_____

20 ⬭ * _____

_____

_____

_____

20 ⬭ * _____

_____

_____

_____

SEPTEMBER

"Almost every wise saying has an opposite one,
no less wise, to balance it."

—*George Santayana*

20 ___ * _____

_____

_____

_____

20 ___ * _____

_____

_____

_____

20 ___ * _____

_____

_____

_____

20 ___ * _____

_____

_____

_____

20 ___ * _____

_____

_____

_____

SEPTEMBER 23

My husband and I both experienced a lot of novelty and challenge in our work—sometimes too much. Would we be happier if our marriage was a refuge of comfort, calm, and order—or should we be more adventurous? On a free night, were we better off reading in bed and going to sleep early, or pushing ourselves to go to a cooking class?

20 ___ * _____

_____

_____

_____

20 ___ * _____

_____

_____

_____

20 ___ * _____

_____

_____

_____

20 ___ * _____

_____

_____

_____

20 ___ * _____

_____

_____

_____

24 SEPTEMBER

Sometimes, it is helpful to introduce an idea to my husband, let it sink in, then raise it another day, instead of bringing it up at thirty-minute intervals, as I'm inclined to do.

20 ___ * _____

_____

_____

20 ___ * _____

_____

_____

20 ___ * _____

_____

_____

20 ___ * _____

_____

_____

20 ___ * _____

_____

_____

SEPTEMBER

"What lies in our power to do, it lies in
our power not to do."

—*Aristotle*

20 ___ * _____

_____

_____

20 ___ * _____

_____

_____

20 ___ * _____

_____

_____

20 ___ * _____

_____

_____

20 ___ * _____

_____

_____

26 SEPTEMBER

Read the manual. Even a small step toward growth—like learning to use a new camera—gives a boost. And eliminating feelings of frustration and incompetence is a happiness-booster, too.

20 ___ * _____

_____

_____

_____

20 ___ * _____

_____

_____

_____

20 ___ * _____

_____

_____

_____

20 ___ * _____

_____

_____

_____

20 ___ * _____

_____

_____

_____

SEPTEMBER

Sometimes, choosing to "feel right" means accepting some "feeling bad." Happiness doesn't always make me *feel* happy; I dislike every step of dealing with yearly flu shots for my family, yet this chore also makes me happy.

20 ___ * _____

20 ___ * _____

20 ___ * _____

20 ___ * _____

20 ___ * _____

28 SEPTEMBER

The aim of a happiness project is not to eliminate all forms of unhappiness from life. Negative emotions—up to a point—can play a very helpful role in a happy life. They're powerful, flashy signs that something isn't right. They often prod you into action.

20____ * _____

_____

_____

_____

20____ * _____

_____

_____

_____

20____ * _____

_____

_____

_____

20____ * _____

_____

_____

_____

20____ * _____

_____

_____

_____

SEPTEMBER

"The important question is not, what will yield
to man a few scattered pleasures, but what will render
his life happy on the whole amount."

—Joseph Addison

20 __ * _____

_____

_____

_____

20 __ * _____

_____

_____

_____

20 __ * _____

_____

_____

_____

20 __ * _____

_____

_____

_____

20 __ * _____

_____

_____

_____

30 SEPTEMBER

One key to happiness is self-knowledge, and yet it's very, very hard to know myself—especially painful aspects that I want to deny. Negative emotions highlight things I try to conceal. For example, when I was thinking of switching careers from law to writing, the uncomfortable emotion of envy helped show me what I really wanted.

20 ___ * _____

_____

_____

20 ___ * _____

_____

_____

20 ___ * _____

_____

_____

20 ___ * _____

_____

_____

20 ___ * _____

_____

_____

OCTOBER

1

There's no one right way to happiness, but only
the way that's right for a particular person—which
is why mindfulness matters so much to happiness.
To be happier, you have to notice what you're doing,
and why, and how it makes you feel.

20 ___ * _____

_____

_____

20 ___ * _____

_____

_____

20 ___ * _____

_____

_____

20 ___ * _____

_____

_____

20 ___ * _____

_____

_____

2 OCTOBER

"If one thinks that one is happy,
that is enough to be happy."

—*Madame de la Fayette*

20 ___ * _____
_____
_____
_____

20 ___ * _____
_____
_____
_____

20 ___ * _____
_____
_____
_____

20 ___ * _____
_____
_____
_____

20 ___ * _____
_____
_____
_____

OCTOBER

To be yourself is the way to happiness, but there is also a sadness to this resolution—the sadness that comes from admitting your limitations, your indifferences, all the things that you wish you were that you will never be. To cram your days full of the things you love, you have to acknowledge the things that play no part in your happiness.

20 ___ * _____

_____

_____

_____

20 ___ * _____

_____

_____

_____

20 ___ * _____

_____

_____

_____

20 ___ * _____

_____

_____

_____

20 ___ * _____

_____

_____

_____

OCTOBER

4

"Whenever we give up, leave behind, and forget
too much, there is always the danger that the things
we have neglected will return with added force."

—*Carl Jung*

20 ⬭ * _____

_____

_____

_____

20 ⬭ * _____

_____

_____

_____

20 ⬭ * _____

_____

_____

_____

20 ⬭ * _____

_____

_____

_____

20 ⬭ * _____

_____

_____

_____

OCTOBER

5

When you are reluctant to take a risk, ask yourself these Five
Fateful Questions: What am I waiting for? What would I do
if I weren't scared? What steps would make things easier?
What would I do if I had all the time and money in the world?
Five years from now, what would I wish I'd done?

20 __ * _____

_____

_____

_____

20 __ * _____

_____

_____

_____

20 __ * _____

_____

_____

_____

20 __ * _____

_____

_____

_____

20 __ * _____

_____

_____

_____

OCTOBER

"Then he rustled his feathers, curved his slender neck, and cried joyfully, from the depths of his heart, 'I never dreamed of such happiness as this, while I was an ugly duckling.'"

—*Hans Christian Andersen,* **Ugly Duckling**

20 ___ * _____

_____

_____

_____

20 ___ * _____

_____

_____

_____

20 ___ * _____

_____

_____

_____

20 ___ * _____

_____

_____

_____

20 ___ * _____

_____

_____

_____

OCTOBER

As part of my happiness project, I devised a set of personal commandments, a list of overarching principles that I use to guide my thoughts and behavior. For instance: enjoy the process, spend out, lighten up, identify the problem, and dig deep.

20 ___ * _____

_____

_____

_____

20 ___ * _____

_____

_____

_____

20 ___ * _____

_____

_____

_____

20 ___ * _____

_____

_____

_____

20 ___ * _____

_____

_____

_____

8 OCTOBER

Controlling my quick irritation and my sharp tongue
was something I struggled with every day. I knew I couldn't
yell or snap my way toward the loving, peaceful, tender
atmosphere that I wanted. Dig deep, dig deep.

20 ___ * _____

_____

_____

_____

20 ___ * _____

_____

_____

_____

20 ___ * _____

_____

_____

_____

20 ___ * _____

_____

_____

_____

20 ___ * _____

_____

_____

_____

OCTOBER

9

"Quiet minds cannot be perplexed or frightened
but go on in fortune or misfortune at their own private
pace, like a clock during a thunderstorm."

—*Robert Louis Stevenson*

20 ___ * _____

_____

_____

20 ___ * _____

_____

_____

20 ___ * _____

_____

_____

20 ___ * _____

_____

_____

20 ___ * _____

_____

_____

10 OCTOBER

It's easier to prevent pain than to squelch it.
Literally and figuratively.

20 ⬭ __ *_____
_____
_____
_____

20 ⬭ __ *_____
_____
_____
_____

20 ⬭ __ *_____
_____
_____
_____

20 ⬭ __ *_____
_____
_____
_____

20 ⬭ __ *_____
_____
_____
_____

OCTOBER

11

"Nothing can make our life, or the lives of other people,
more beautiful than perpetual kindness."

—*Leo Tolstoy*

20 ___ * _____

_____

_____

20 ___ * _____

_____

_____

20 ___ * _____

_____

_____

20 ___ * _____

_____

_____

20 ___ * _____

_____

_____

12 OCTOBER

Happy people volunteer more, give away more money,
and naturally take an interest in others.

20 ___ * _____

_____

_____

_____

20 ___ * _____

_____

_____

_____

20 ___ * _____

_____

_____

_____

20 ___ * _____

_____

_____

_____

20 ___ * _____

_____

_____

_____

OCTOBER

13

"He who would bring home the wealth of the Indies
must carry the wealth of the Indies with him."

—*Samuel Johnson*

20 ___ * _____

_____

_____

20 ___ * _____

_____

_____

_____

20 ___ * _____

_____

_____

20 ___ * _____

_____

_____

20 ___ * _____

_____

_____

_____

14 OCTOBER

"All wisdom is not new wisdom."

—Winston Churchill

20 ___ * _____

_____

_____

_____

20 ___ * _____

_____

_____

_____

20 ___ * _____

_____

_____

_____

20 ___ * _____

_____

_____

_____

20 ___ * _____

_____

_____

_____

OCTOBER 15

"Each time of life has its own kind of love."

—*Leo Tolstoy*

20 ___ * _____

_____

_____

20 ___ * _____

_____

_____

20 ___ * _____

_____

_____

20 ___ * _____

_____

_____

20 ___ * _____

_____

_____

16 OCTOBER

Spending time with children allows us to experience our own sincere enjoyment of activities—going to the circus, decorating cookies, making balloon animals—that we wouldn't undertake on our own.

20 ___ * _____

_____

_____

_____

20 ___ * _____

_____

_____

_____

20 ___ * _____

_____

_____

_____

20 ___ * _____

_____

_____

_____

20 ___ * _____

_____

_____

_____

OCTOBER 17

There are three categories of fun: challenging fun,
the most demanding type of fun; accommodating fun,
which also takes effort; and relaxing fun, which
requires no skill or action.

20 ___ * _____

_____

_____

_____

20 ___ * _____

_____

_____

_____

20 ___ * _____

_____

_____

_____

20 ___ * _____

_____

_____

_____

20 ___ * _____

_____

_____

_____

18

OCTOBER

Fun is enjoyable because you don't have to worry about results. You can strive for triumph or you can putter around, tinker, and explore, without worrying about efficiency or outcomes.

20 ___ * _____

_____

_____

_____

20 ___ * _____

_____

_____

_____

20 ___ * _____

_____

_____

_____

20 ___ * _____

_____

_____

_____

20 ___ * _____

_____

_____

_____

OCTOBER

19

SECRET OF ADULTHOOD: If you're too tired to do anything except watch television or cruise the Internet, go to sleep.

20 __ * _____

_____

_____

20 __ * _____

_____

_____

20 __ * _____

_____

_____

20 __ * _____

_____

_____

20 __ * _____

_____

_____

20 OCTOBER

"Do not spoil what you have by desiring what you have not; but remember that what you now have was once among the things you only hoped for."

—*Epicurus*

20 ⬤ * _____

_____

_____

_____

20 ⬤ * _____

_____

_____

_____

20 ⬤ * _____

_____

_____

_____

20 ⬤ * _____

_____

_____

_____

20 ⬤ * _____

_____

_____

_____

OCTOBER

21

"As soon as you stop wanting something you get it.
I've found that to be absolutely axiomatic."

—*Andy Warhol*

20 ⬤ * _____

_____

_____

_____

20 ⬤ * _____

_____

_____

_____

20 ⬤ * _____

_____

_____

_____

20 ⬤ * _____

_____

_____

_____

20 ⬤ * _____

_____

_____

_____

22 OCTOBER

It's easy to think that if you have something
you love or there is something you want,
you'll be even happier with more.

20 ___ * _____

_____

_____

_____

20 ___ * _____

_____

_____

_____

20 ___ * _____

_____

_____

_____

20 ___ * _____

_____

_____

_____

20 ___ * _____

_____

_____

_____

OCTOBER

23

SECRETS OF ADULTHOOD: Clear areas stay clear, and messy areas become messier. Surfaces should be used for activities, not storage.

20 __ * _____

_____

_____

20 __ * _____

_____

_____

20 __ * _____

_____

_____

20 __ * _____

_____

_____

20 __ * _____

_____

_____

_____

24 OCTOBER

One very effective way to complete a project is
to abandon it; a source of clutter in your home,
and worse, in your mind, is the uncomfortable
presence of unfinished projects.

20 ___ * _____

_____

_____

_____

20 ___ * _____

_____

_____

_____

20 ___ * _____

_____

_____

_____

20 ___ * _____

_____

_____

_____

20 ___ * _____

_____

_____

_____

OCTOBER

25

Beware of problem items, such as broken objects, things that seem potentially useful but never get used, and duplicates. How many spare glass salsa jars can you use?

20 ___ * _____

_____

_____

20 ___ * _____

_____

_____

20 ___ * _____

_____

_____

20 ___ * _____

_____

_____

20 ___ * _____

_____

_____

26 OCTOBER

Often, the things I want to "save" make no sense.
What's the point of fancy bath gel if it never leaves
the container? Why was I "saving" those colorful
tin trays from my grandmother?

20 ⬭ * _____

_____

_____

_____

20 ⬭ * _____

_____

_____

_____

20 ⬭ * _____

_____

_____

_____

20 ⬭ * _____

_____

_____

_____

20 ⬭ * _____

_____

_____

_____

OCTOBER

27

My daughter didn't use her tiny animal ink stamps anymore, and I didn't use the gorgeously bright vintage paper hats that my mother gave me—and yet, these things were precious in their way. I wanted my home to be filled with objects of symbolic and sentimental attraction as well as practical value.

20 ___ * _____

_____

_____

_____

20 ___ * _____

_____

_____

_____

20 ___ * _____

_____

_____

_____

20 ___ * _____

_____

_____

_____

20 ___ * _____

_____

_____

_____

28 OCTOBER

Build a treasure house of happy memories.
Find ways to memorialize little family jokes and funny
incidents, birthday parties, and holiday dinners.

20 ___ * _____

_____

_____

_____

20 ___ * _____

_____

_____

_____

20 ___ * _____

_____

_____

_____

20 ___ * _____

_____

_____

_____

20 ___ * _____

_____

_____

_____

OCTOBER

29

The approach of Halloween meant it was time to decorate our apartment, and I felt the familiar battle in my soul. Part of me wanted to simplify my life, eliminate work, and ignore our boxes of decorations. But while I felt the urge to do as little as possible, I knew I was happier when I made efforts that marked the seasons.

20 ___ * _____

_____

_____

20 ___ * _____

_____

_____

_____

20 ___ * _____

_____

_____

20 ___ * _____

_____

_____

20 ___ * _____

_____

_____

_____

30 OCTOBER

"It is impossible to win the great prizes of life without running risks, and the greatest of all prizes are those connected with the home."

—*Theodore Roosevelt*

20 ___ * _____

_____

_____

_____

20 ___ * _____

_____

_____

_____

20 ___ * _____

_____

_____

_____

20 ___ * _____

_____

_____

_____

20 ___ * _____

_____

_____

_____

OCTOBER

Happiness has a surprisingly mixed reputation.
There is an assumption that happy people strike
others as annoying and shallow, but in fact,
they tend to attract others.

20 __ * _____

_____

_____

_____

20 __ * _____

_____

_____

_____

20 __ * _____

_____

_____

_____

20 __ * _____

_____

_____

_____

20 __ * _____

_____

_____

_____

1

NOVEMBER

I vowed to resist happiness leeches and to free
myself from the nefarious influence of anyone who
was sucking the happiness out of me.

20＿＿ *_____

_____

_____

_____

20＿＿ *_____

_____

_____

_____

20＿＿ *_____

_____

_____

_____

20＿＿ *_____

_____

_____

_____

20＿＿ *_____

_____

_____

_____

NOVEMBER

Avoid being alone with a happiness leech. The presence
of other people often dilutes his or her power.

20 ___ * _____

_____

_____

_____

20 ___ * _____

_____

_____

_____

20 ___ * _____

_____

_____

_____

20 ___ * _____

_____

_____

_____

20 ___ * _____

_____

_____

_____

NOVEMBER

Instead of contradicting pessimistic or negative statements, acknowledge them. Happiness leeches are often less emphatic when they feel that others recognize their views.

20 ___ * _____

_____

_____

_____

20 ___ * _____

_____

_____

_____

20 ___ * _____

_____

_____

_____

20 ___ * _____

_____

_____

_____

20 ___ * _____

_____

_____

_____

NOVEMBER

4

People of pronounced positivity or negativity may polarize each other. When the Tigger and the Eeyore meet, the Tigger becomes ever more insistently cheery, and the Eeyore becomes more negative, to resist each other's influence. In a frustrating cycle, they oppose and exhaust each other.

20 ___ * _____

_____

_____

20 ___ * _____

_____

_____

20 ___ * _____

_____

_____

20 ___ * _____

_____

_____

20 ___ * _____

_____

_____

5 NOVEMBER

So how can Tiggers and Eeyores cope with each other? Acknowledging someone else's point of view, without trying to correct or deny it, slackens the tension, and in any event, it's rare for either side to make a convert. Tiggers and Eeyores alike are proud of their identities; they aren't going to be talked out of their positions.

20 ⬭ * _____

_____

_____

_____

20 ⬭ * _____

_____

_____

_____

20 ⬭ * _____

_____

_____

_____

20 ⬭ * _____

_____

_____

_____

20 ⬭ * _____

_____

_____

_____

NOVEMBER

Act the way I want to feel; behave the way I want to behave.
Too often, when I find myself around a happiness leech,
I ape that behavior—complaining more, making sharper
criticisms. I want to live up to my own standards.

20 ___ * _____

_____

_____

_____

20 ___ * _____

_____

_____

_____

20 ___ * _____

_____

_____

_____

20 ___ * _____

_____

_____

_____

20 ___ * _____

_____

_____

_____

7 NOVEMBER

"Optimism is true moral courage."

—*Ernest Shackleton*

20 ⬭ * _____

_____

_____

_____

20 ⬭ * _____

_____

_____

_____

20 ⬭ * _____

_____

_____

_____

20 ⬭ * _____

_____

_____

_____

20 ⬭ * _____

_____

_____

_____

NOVEMBER

Studies show that celebrating good news, and showing
the happiness you feel in your partner's accomplishments,
small and large, strengthens a relationship. Being silently
supportive isn't very effective.

20 ___ * _____

_____

_____

20 ___ * _____

_____

_____

20 ___ * _____

_____

_____

20 ___ * _____

_____

_____

20 ___ * _____

_____

_____

NOVEMBER

When I speak to other people about my husband,
whether he is present or not, I say only good things—
rather than complaining or criticizing.

20 ___ * _____
_____
_____
_____

20 ___ * _____
_____
_____
_____

20 ___ * _____
_____
_____
_____

20 ___ * _____
_____
_____
_____

20 ___ * _____
_____
_____
_____

NOVEMBER

"The grand essentials to happiness in this life are something to do, something to love, and something to hope for."

—*Joseph Addison*

20 ___ * _____

_____

_____

20 ___ * _____

_____

_____

20 ___ * _____

_____

_____

20 ___ * _____

_____

_____

20 ___ * _____

_____

_____

11 NOVEMBER

Some people feel overwhelmed by the question "What's your passion?" It seems huge and unanswerable. If so, a useful clue to finding an occupation to pursue, whether for work or play, is identifying what you *do*. What do you actually *do*?

20 ___ * _____

_____

_____

_____

20 ___ * _____

_____

_____

_____

20 ___ * _____

_____

_____

_____

20 ___ * _____

_____

_____

_____

20 ___ * _____

_____

_____

_____

NOVEMBER

12

Any single happy experience may be
amplified or minimized, depending on how
much attention is focused on it.

20 ___ * _____

_____

_____

_____

20 ___ * _____

_____

_____

_____

20 ___ * _____

_____

_____

_____

20 ___ * _____

_____

_____

_____

20 ___ * _____

_____

_____

_____

13 NOVEMBER

"That is happiness; to be dissolved into
something complete and great."

—*Willa Cather*

20 ___ * _____
_____
_____
_____

20 ___ * _____
_____
_____
_____

20 ___ * _____
_____
_____
_____

20 ___ * _____
_____
_____
_____

20 ___ * _____
_____
_____
_____

NOVEMBER

When I acknowledged my true likes and dislikes,
instead of being distracted by what I *wished*
I liked or thought I *ought* to like, I started
a children's literature reading group.

20 ⬭ * _____

_____

_____

20 ⬭ * _____

_____

_____

20 ⬭ * _____

_____

_____

20 ⬭ * _____

_____

_____

20 ⬭ * _____

_____

_____

15 NOVEMBER

Belonging to a children's literature reading group ensured that I made time in my schedule to read and discuss these books. I decided to make a physical place for this passion, as well; I reorganized some bookcases to make a Shrine to Children's Literature.

20 ⬭ * _____

_____

_____

_____

20 ⬭ * _____

_____

_____

_____

20 ⬭ * _____

_____

_____

_____

20 ⬭ * _____

_____

_____

_____

20 ⬭ * _____

_____

_____

_____

NOVEMBER 16

If you don't know what to do for fun, ask yourself,
"What did I enjoy doing when I was ten years old?"
An activity that you enjoyed as a ten-year-old is
probably something you would enjoy doing now.

20 ___ * _____

_____

_____

20 ___ * _____

_____

_____

20 ___ * _____

_____

_____

20 ___ * _____

_____

_____

20 ___ * _____

_____

_____

17 NOVEMBER

"Children think not of what is past, nor what is to come,
but enjoy the present time, which few of us do."

—*Jean de La Bruyère*

20 ___ * _____

_____

_____

_____

20 ___ * _____

_____

_____

_____

20 ___ * _____

_____

_____

_____

20 ___ * _____

_____

_____

_____

20 ___ * _____

_____

_____

_____

NOVEMBER

Make time for passion. Consider it a real priority instead of an "extra" to be squeezed in when you have some free time. You may never have any free time.

20 ___ * _____

_____

_____

20 ___ * _____

_____

_____

20 ___ * _____

_____

_____

20 ___ * _____

_____

_____

20 ___ * _____

_____

_____

19 NOVEMBER

If you're pursuing a challenging goal, gather people around you who share your interest and can give you support and encouragement.

20 ⬤ * _____
_____
_____
_____

20 ⬤ * _____
_____
_____
_____

20 ⬤ * _____
_____
_____
_____

20 ⬤ * _____
_____
_____
_____

20 ⬤ * _____
_____
_____
_____

NOVEMBER

One of the most generous acts is to help
someone to *think big*. Words of enthusiasm and
confidence from a friend can inspire a person
to tackle an ambitious goal.

20 ___ * _____

_____

_____

20 ___ * _____

_____

_____

20 ___ * _____

_____

_____

20 ___ * _____

_____

_____

20 ___ * _____

_____

_____

21 NOVEMBER

Show support for a friend who has unhappy news, and also for a friend who has happy news. It's sometimes more challenging to be supportive in the face of good fortune.

20 ___ * _____

_____

_____

_____

20 ___ * _____

_____

_____

_____

20 ___ * _____

_____

_____

_____

20 ___ * _____

_____

_____

_____

20 ___ * _____

_____

_____

_____

NOVEMBER

"We seldom think of what we have but always of what we lack."

— *Schopenhauer*

20 ___ * _____

_____

_____

_____

20 ___ * _____

_____

_____

_____

20 ___ * _____

_____

_____

_____

20 ___ * _____

_____

_____

_____

20 ___ * _____

_____

_____

_____

"He was like a man owning a piece of ground
in which, unknown to himself, a treasure lay buried.
You would not call such a man rich, neither would I
call happy the man who is so without realizing it."

—*Eugène Delacroix*

20 ____ * _____

_____

_____

_____

20 ____ * _____

_____

_____

_____

20 ____ * _____

_____

_____

_____

20 ____ * _____

_____

_____

_____

20 ____ * _____

_____

_____

_____

NOVEMBER

As the weather becomes colder and drearier, our sturdy,
snug apartment seems even more comfortable. Sitting
inside the warm, pleasant kitchen while icy rain beats
against the window, I feel the wordless contentment of
a horse in a stable or a wren in a birdhouse.

20 ___ * _____

_____

_____

_____

20 ___ * _____

_____

_____

_____

20 ___ * _____

_____

_____

_____

20 ___ * _____

_____

_____

_____

20 ___ * _____

_____

_____

_____

25 NOVEMBER

As I walked in the door of my building, I thought, yet again, of how much I wanted to make my home a haven of comfort, warmth, and tenderness. We were in the rush hour of life, and everything was moving so quickly, and every day seemed so crowded—more reason to remember to slow down, stay patient, take photographs, and play Hide and Seek.

20 ___ * _____

_____

_____

_____

20 ___ * _____

_____

_____

_____

20 ___ * _____

_____

_____

_____

20 ___ * _____

_____

_____

_____

20 ___ * _____

_____

_____

_____

NOVEMBER

All of my happiness-project resolutions are actions that I can do myself; however, somewhat to my surprise, we all began to follow the resolution to give warm greetings and farewells. The more we did it, the more it became a habit. As a consequence, each day, several times, we had moments of real connection among all members of our family.

20 ____ * _____

_____

_____

_____

20 ____ * _____

_____

_____

_____

20 ____ * _____

_____

_____

_____

20 ____ * _____

_____

_____

_____

20 ____ * _____

_____

_____

_____

27   **NOVEMBER**

You get more of what you have. When you feel friendly,
people want to be your friend. When you feel attractive,
people are attracted to you. When you feel loving, others act
lovingly toward you. This truth is cruel because so often,
you want others to give you what you lack.

20 ⬭ * _____

_____

_____

_____

20 ⬭ * _____

_____

_____

_____

20 ⬭ * _____

_____

_____

_____

20 ⬭ * _____

_____

_____

_____

20 ⬭ * _____

_____

_____

_____

NOVEMBER 28

If I want a household with an affectionate, encouraging,
and playful atmosphere, that's the spirit *I* must bring
with me every time I step out of the elevator.

20 __ * _____

_____

_____

20 __ * _____

_____

_____

20 __ * _____

_____

_____

20 __ * _____

_____

_____

20 __ * _____

_____

_____

29 NOVEMBER

It's from the experience of a particular individual that I learn most about *myself*—even if we two seem to have nothing in common. Some of my own best guides, it happens, continue to be an argumentative, procrastinating lexicographer, and a nun who spent more than a third of her short life in a cloistered convent.

20 ___ * _____

_____

_____

_____

20 ___ * _____

_____

_____

_____

20 ___ * _____

_____

_____

_____

20 ___ * _____

_____

_____

_____

20 ___ * _____

_____

_____

_____

NOVEMBER 30

A Zen koan holds "If you meet the Buddha on the road, kill him." What does that mean? Mere emulation—even emulation of a spiritual master like the Buddha—wasn't the way to happiness. You have to follow what is true for *you*.

20 ___ * _____

_____

_____

20 ___ * _____

_____

_____

20 ___ * _____

_____

_____

20 ___ * _____

_____

_____

20 ___ * _____

_____

_____

1 DECEMBER

Mother Teresa advised, "Find your own Calcutta," meaning, instead of grabbing on to the mission that she'd made famous, people should find their own causes. Just as she'd experienced a "call within a call" that guided her to a particular kind of work, others should discover what cause moves them to action, and where their skills could be useful.

20___ * _____

_____

_____

_____

20___ * _____

_____

_____

_____

20___ * _____

_____

_____

_____

20___ * _____

_____

_____

_____

20___ * _____

_____

_____

_____

DECEMBER

2

A "moment of obligation" is the moment when you think—hey, someone should really try to improve this situation, and you realize, *I'm* the one who should do something. *Me.*

20 ___ * _____

_____

_____

_____

20 ___ * _____

_____

_____

_____

20 ___ * _____

_____

_____

_____

20 ___ * _____

_____

_____

_____

20 ___ * _____

_____

_____

_____

3 DECEMBER

Be selfless, if only for selfish reasons. And it's not just that helpful people also tend to be healthier and happier; helping others *causes* happiness.

20 ___ * _____

_____

_____

_____

20 ___ * _____

_____

_____

_____

20 ___ * _____

_____

_____

_____

20 ___ * _____

_____

_____

_____

20 ___ * _____

_____

_____

_____

DECEMBER

We don't get healthy self-esteem from constantly telling ourselves how great we are, or even from other people telling us how great we are. We get healthy self-esteem from behaving in ways that we find worthy of our own respect—such as helping other people.

20 ___ * _____

_____

_____

20 ___ * _____

_____

_____

20 ___ * _____

_____

_____

20 ___ * _____

_____

_____

20 ___ * _____

_____

_____

_____

5 DECEMBER

"If better were within, better would come out."

—*Simon Patrick*

20 ___ * _____

_____

_____

_____

20 ___ * _____

_____

_____

_____

20 ___ * _____

_____

_____

_____

20 ___ * _____

_____

_____

_____

20 ___ * _____

_____

_____

_____

DECEMBER

"Everyone thinks of changing the world, but no
one thinks of changing himself."

— *Leo Tolstoy*

20 ___ * _____

_____

_____

20 ___ * _____

_____

_____

20 ___ * _____

_____

_____

20 ___ * _____

_____

_____

20 ___ * _____

_____

_____

7 DECEMBER

"Choose which seems best and, in the doing,
it will become agreeable and easy."

—*Pythagoras*

20 ___ * _____

_____

_____

_____

20 ___ * _____

_____

_____

_____

20 ___ * _____

_____

_____

_____

20 ___ * _____

_____

_____

_____

20 ___ * _____

_____

_____

_____

DECEMBER

Often, making a purchase just makes clutter worse, but then again, sometimes a purchase helps. As an *underbuyer*, I often decide, "Maybe we don't really need this," or "I'll buy this some other time." I suffer needless annoyance because I don't have what I need or I'm using something that isn't exactly suitable.

20 ___ * _____

_____

_____

20 ___ * _____

_____

_____

20 ___ * _____

_____

_____

20 ___ * _____

_____

_____

20 ___ * _____

_____

_____

DECEMBER

Overbuyers tell themselves, "We can probably use that," "This might come in handy, someday," "Why not get one in every color?" Overbuyers suffer needless annoyance because of the time, money, energy, and space necessary to support their overbuying.

20 ⬭ * _____

_____

_____

_____

20 ⬭ * _____

_____

_____

_____

20 ⬭ * _____

_____

_____

_____

20 ⬭ * _____

_____

_____

_____

20 ⬭ * _____

_____

_____

_____

DECEMBER 10

Some research suggests that spending money on an experience brings more happiness than buying a possession, but the line between possessions and experiences isn't always simple to draw. Many wonderful experiences require, or are enhanced by, possessions.

20 __ * _____

_____

_____

20 __ * _____

_____

_____

20 __ * _____

_____

_____

20 __ * _____

_____

_____

20 __ * _____

_____

_____

11 DECEMBER

For many people, shopping itself is an enjoyable
experience; acquisition of possessions is part
of the fun, but not all of the fun.

20 ⬤ * _____

_____

_____

_____

20 ⬤ * _____

_____

_____

_____

20 ⬤ * _____

_____

_____

_____

20 ⬤ * _____

_____

_____

_____

20 ⬤ * _____

_____

_____

_____

DECEMBER

12

We often deny the importance of possessions, or feel
embarrassed by our enthusiasm for them, but the desire
to possess has roots very deep in human nature.

20 ___ * _____

_____

_____

20 ___ * _____

_____

_____

20 ___ * _____

_____

_____

20 ___ * _____

_____

_____

20 ___ * _____

_____

_____

13 DECEMBER

"To be without some of the things you want is
an indispensable part of happiness."

—*Bertrand Russell*

20 ___ * _____

_____

_____

_____

20 ___ * _____

_____

_____

_____

20 ___ * _____

_____

_____

_____

20 ___ * _____

_____

_____

_____

20 ___ * _____

_____

_____

_____

DECEMBER 14

For better or worse, buying things (or photographing them, cataloging them, or writing reviews about them) is a way to engage with the world. When we're interested in something, we often express that interest by researching, shopping, buying, and collecting.

20 ___ * _____

_____

_____

_____

20 ___ * _____

_____

_____

_____

20 ___ * _____

_____

_____

_____

20 ___ * _____

_____

_____

_____

20 ___ * _____

_____

_____

_____

15 DECEMBER

"The real pleasure-seeking is the combination of luxury and austerity in such a way that the luxury can really be felt."

— *G.K. Chesterton*

20 ___ * _____

_____

_____

_____

20 ___ * _____

_____

_____

_____

20 ___ * _____

_____

_____

_____

20 ___ * _____

_____

_____

_____

20 ___ * _____

_____

_____

_____

DECEMBER 16

Was it possible to be happy with very few possessions?
Yes. Were some people happier when they owned almost
nothing? Yes. But for most people, including me,
possessions, wisely chosen, could be a boon to happiness.

20 ___ * _____

_____

_____

20 ___ * _____

_____

_____

20 ___ * _____

_____

_____

20 ___ * _____

_____

_____

20 ___ * _____

_____

_____

17 DECEMBER

While I love the fun of the holidays, I dread its sugary temptations. If I overindulge, I feel guilty and irritable. A solution struck me: "Maybe I should just decide to eat *not one more sweet thing* until January." And the minute I decided to do that, I felt a huge sense of relief. It would be much easier for me to eat *no* sweets than to eat a *few* sweets.

20 ___ * _____

_____

_____

_____

20 ___ * _____

_____

_____

_____

20 ___ * _____

_____

_____

_____

20 ___ * _____

_____

_____

_____

20 ___ * _____

_____

_____

_____

DECEMBER 18

Research has shown that we start each day with a limited amount of self-control, and as we use it, we gradually deplete it. As our self-control gets used up, we find it harder to resist new temptations.

20 ___ * _____

_____

_____

_____

20 ___ * _____

_____

_____

_____

20 ___ * _____

_____

_____

_____

20 ___ * _____

_____

_____

_____

20 ___ * _____

_____

_____

_____

19 DECEMBER

Employ the weapon of *convenience* by making it easy to do the things you want to do. For example, putting on your gym clothes as soon as you get up in the morning will make it easier to get yourself to the gym.

20 ___ * _____

_____

_____

_____

20 ___ * _____

_____

_____

_____

20 ___ * _____

_____

_____

_____

20 ___ * _____

_____

_____

_____

20 ___ * _____

_____

_____

_____

DECEMBER 20

"Abstainers" find it much easier to abstain than
to indulge moderately. They are not tempted by things
that they've decided are off-limits, but once they start
something, they have trouble stopping.

20 ___ * _____

_____

_____

_____

20 ___ * _____

_____

_____

_____

20 ___ * _____

_____

_____

_____

20 ___ * _____

_____

_____

_____

20 ___ * _____

_____

_____

_____

21 | **DECEMBER**

If I never do something, it requires *no*
self-control for me; if I do something sometimes,
it requires *enormous* self-control.

20 ___ * _____

_____

_____

_____

20 ___ * _____

_____

_____

_____

20 ___ * _____

_____

_____

_____

20 ___ * _____

_____

_____

_____

20 ___ * _____

_____

_____

_____

DECEMBER

"Moderators," by contrast, do better when they act with moderation, because they feel trapped and rebellious at the thought of "never" getting or doing something. Occasional indulgence heightens their pleasure and strengthens their resolve.

20 ___ * _____

_____

_____

_____

20 ___ * _____

_____

_____

_____

20 ___ * _____

_____

_____

_____

20 ___ * _____

_____

_____

_____

20 ___ * _____

_____

_____

_____

23 DECEMBER

"One of the secrets of a happy life
is continuous small treats."

—*Iris Murdoch*

20 ___ * _____

_____

_____

_____

20 ___ * _____

_____

_____

_____

20 ___ * _____

_____

_____

_____

20 ___ * _____

_____

_____

_____

20 ___ * _____

_____

_____

_____

DECEMBER

24

"No man knows how bad he is till he has tried very hard to be good. . . . Only those who try to resist temptation know how strong it is."

—*C.S. Lewis*

20 ___ * _____

_____

_____

_____

20 ___ * _____

_____

_____

_____

20 ___ * _____

_____

_____

_____

20 ___ * _____

_____

_____

_____

20 ___ * _____

_____

_____

_____

25 DECEMBER

My parents have saved many of my favorite childhood playthings, and re-discovering these old toys is one of the traditions that my daughters and I enjoy most about our regular visits. A key childhood memory for my children, I knew, would be Christmas in Kansas City.

20 __ * _____

_____

_____

_____

20 __ * _____

_____

_____

_____

20 __ * _____

_____

_____

_____

20 __ * _____

_____

_____

_____

20 __ * _____

_____

_____

_____

DECEMBER

"'Now run along and play, but don't get into trouble.' George promised to be good. But it is easy for little monkeys to forget."

—*H.A. Rey*, **Curious George**

20 ⬤__ *_____

_____

_____

_____

20 ⬤__ *_____

_____

_____

_____

20 ⬤__ *_____

_____

_____

_____

20 ⬤__ *_____

_____

_____

_____

20 ⬤__ *_____

_____

_____

_____

27 DECEMBER

"The moon is high. The sea is deep.
They rock and rock and rock to sleep."

— Sandra Boynton, **The Going to Bed Book**

20 ___ * _____

_____

_____

_____

20 ___ * _____

_____

_____

_____

20 ___ * _____

_____

_____

_____

20 ___ * _____

_____

_____

_____

20 ___ * _____

_____

_____

_____

DECEMBER 28

One of the persistent follies of human nature is to imagine true happiness is just out of reach. The "arrival fallacy" describes our tendency to believe that once we arrive at a particular destination, *then* we'll be happy.

20 ⬭ * _____

_____

_____

_____

20 ⬭ * _____

_____

_____

_____

20 ⬭ * _____

_____

_____

_____

20 ⬭ * _____

_____

_____

_____

20 ⬭ * _____

_____

_____

_____

29 DECEMBER

"Everything that frees our spirit without
giving us control of ourselves is ruinous."

—*Goethe*

20 ⬭ _ _ * _____

_____

_____

_____

20 ⬭ _ _ * _____

_____

_____

_____

20 ⬭ _ _ * _____

_____

_____

_____

20 ⬭ _ _ * _____

_____

_____

_____

20 ⬭ _ _ * _____

_____

_____

_____

DECEMBER

Throughout about my life, I've experienced a skipping,
a feeling of jumping from prologue to epilogue without
ever feeling that I'm at the center of time. "It's too soon for
that" I'd think, then suddenly, overnight, "It's too late
for that." I didn't want to come to the end of my life and
wish I'd paid more attention along the way.

20 ⬤ * _____

_____

_____

_____

20 ⬤ * _____

_____

_____

_____

20 ⬤ * _____

_____

_____

_____

20 ⬤ * _____

_____

_____

_____

20 ⬤ * _____

_____

_____

_____

31 DECEMBER

As I turn the key and push open the front door,
as I cross the threshold, I think how breathtaking,
how fleeting, how precious is my ordinary day.
Now is now. *Here* is my treasure.

20 ___ * _____

_____

_____

_____

20 ___ * _____

_____

_____

_____

20 ___ * _____

_____

_____

_____

20 ___ * _____

_____

_____

_____

20 ___ * _____

_____

_____

_____